"Navigating change is the hardest task that leaders and managers face. Karen Golden-Biddle is here to help. As one of the world's foremost experts on change, she's written a book that is an accessible, actionable resource for finding your way through the fog."

Adam Grant, #1 New York Times *bestselling author of HIDDEN POTENTIAL and THINK AGAIN, and host of the podcast WorkLife*

"You have heard the phrase, 'Embrace the unexpected.' The puzzle remains, as a leader or manager, how do you recognize and make good use of the unexpected in a way that delivers results and positive change for your organization? *The Untapped Power of Discovery* is a unique guide to helping you understand and make good use of unexpected developments and convert them into a capacity for discovery. This focus on the process of discovery produces critical new insights about how to effectively lead during a time of unprecedented change."

Jane Dutton, *Robert L. Kahn Distinguished University Professor Emerita, University of Michigan*

"In a world full of uncertainty and surprises, Karen Golden-Biddle uses extensive research and compelling stories to teach us the overlooked practice of discovery. Readers will have many "ahas" on their way to learning how to more effectively innovate, solve difficult problems and advance in their careers."

Scott Sonenshein, *bestselling author of STRETCH and co-author (with Marie Kondo) of JOY AT WORK*

"This book will benefit any leader concerned about the failure of imagination in their company. Drawing on a wide variety of vivid cases, Golden-Biddle provides a tool-kit to jumpstart discovery in your company and using surprise and doubt are the doorways to lasting change."

Hayagreeva Rao, *Atholl McBean Professor of Organizational Behavior, Graduate School of Business, Stanford University, and co-author (with Robert I. Sutton) of SCALING UP EXCELLENCE and THE FRICTION PROJECT*

"I sat down to start reading this book and couldn't put it down until I finished. This creative and very gripping book helps readers discover quite a lot. It conveys crucial insights by means of true examples of very ambitious change projects, and demonstrates in practice its underlying conceptual message. The examples in each chapter show not only what three-pronged discovery processes mean in practice, but also what the courage to carry them out as an organizational leader involves. The questions at the end of each chapter engage readers, making the experience of reading the book more than just seeing what others have done.

The book conveys beautifully both the temporariness of our knowledge and the worth of temporary unknowing. It conveys the value of being nervous and hesitant, at least with respect to the tools we use. Further, it not only discusses but also shows in practice, the profound importance of respect for people that change agents and other leaders often ignore—such as children, hospital patients, homeless people, village elders, low level employees in organizations. Most books about change do not even acknowledge the importance of such people, let alone incorporate them in creative processes. Finally, the very helpful figure that summarizes each chapter also ties the chapters together very well.

This is a beautifully written book. I hope that it will lead readers to experience some doubt about admonitions for change they have previously read, and point them towards important new possibilities that await creation."

Jean Bartunek, *Robert A. and Evelyn J. Ferris Chair and Professor of Management and Organization, Carroll School of Management, Boston College*

"We must embrace change to achieve success in organizations and have a fulfilling life. Using stories and research, Karen Golden-Biddle provides a compelling framework with actionable strategies to integrate discovery for change with innovative impact."

Kenneth W. Freeman, *Boston University interim president, previously Chairman & CEO of Quest Diagnostics and Partner at KKR*

The Untapped Power of Discovery

Despite being a game-changer in powering human growth, discovery remains a mystery. How can it produce *ahas* and insights to meet the challenge of new realities and reimagine organizational management?

This book lays out a process of inquiry that drives belief change and leads to discoveries, empowering leaders, groups, and the organization with a powerful tool for navigating an uncertain future. Discovery lights the intellectual spark for every breakthrough in science, technology, pharmaceuticals, and more—but fear and inertia can harden beliefs and practices that no longer fit the new realities. To counter this, discovery can be cultivated rather than suppressed, using a new, three-phase process, a management practice that consistently generates the *ahas* and insights that underpin all transformation. Based on years of research and real-world observation, this book inspires and equips leaders at all levels to champion this discovery process and fuel genuine, sustained change in their communities and organizations.

Accompanied by a website that includes proprietary tools, audio and video clips, and a downloadable workbook, this book is an enriching resource for current and aspiring leaders and managers across industries, as well as management consultants, HR professionals, corporate educators, and business students.

Karen Golden-Biddle is an organizational ethnographer whose award-winning research illuminates the connection between discovery and organizational change. She is committed to supporting leaders' efforts to cultivate discovery as a conscious practice. Karen's work has appeared in numerous peer-reviewed publications, including the *Academy of Management Journal* and *Organization Science*. She received her PhD and MBA from Case Western Reserve University and BA from Denison University. Karen is Professor of Management and Organizations, emerita, Questrom School of Business at Boston University, and Fellow of the Academy of Management.

The Untapped Power of Discovery
How to Create Change That Inspires a Better Future

Karen Golden-Biddle

Designed cover image: © Getty

First published 2024
by Routledge
605 Third Avenue, New York, NY 10158

and by Routledge
4 Park Square, Milton Park, Abingdon, Oxon, OX14 4RN

Routledge is an imprint of the Taylor & Francis Group, an informa business

© 2024 Karen Golden-Biddle

The right of Karen Golden-Biddle to be identified as author of this work has been asserted in accordance with sections 77 and 78 of the Copyright, Designs and Patents Act 1988.

All rights reserved. No part of this book may be reprinted or reproduced or utilised in any form or by any electronic, mechanical, or other means, now known or hereafter invented, including photocopying and recording, or in any information storage or retrieval system, without permission in writing from the publishers.

Trademark notice: Product or corporate names may be trademarks or registered trademarks, and are used only for identification and explanation without intent to infringe.

Library of Congress Cataloging-in-Publication Data
Names: Golden-Biddle, Karen, author.
Title: The Untapped Power of Discovery : How To Create Change
   That Inspires a Better Future / Karen Golden-Biddle.
Description: New York, NY : Routledge, 2024. | Includes bibliographical
   references and index.
Identifiers: LCCN 2024015476 (print) | LCCN 2024015477 (ebook) |
   ISBN 9781032845340 (hardback) | ISBN 9781032845319 (paperback) |
   ISBN 9781003513681 (ebook)
Subjects: LCSH: Creative ability in business. | Learning by discovery. | Leadership.
Classification: LCC HD53 .G65 2024 (print) | LCC HD53 (ebook) |
   DDC 658.4/063—dc23/eng/20240404
LC record available at https://lccn.loc.gov/2024015476
LC ebook record available at https://lccn.loc.gov/2024015477

ISBN: 978-1-032-84534-0 (hbk)
ISBN: 978-1-032-84531-9 (pbk)
ISBN: 978-1-003-51368-1 (ebk)

DOI: 10.4324/9781003513681

Typeset in Sabon
by Apex CoVantage, LLC

Please access accompanying online material: https://karengolden-biddle.com/

For Mark

Contents

Acknowledgments — xi

Introduction — 1

1. Suppressing Discovery — 8
2. Discovery as a Process — 28
3. Capitalizing on Surprise — 45
4. Harnessing Genuine Doubt — 62
5. Launching New Ways — 82
6. Building Capacity for Discovery — 99
7. Amplifying Discovery — 117
8. Discovery's Impact on Change Management — 136

Index — 145

Acknowledgments

As I sit down to write these acknowledgements, the many, many people who have supported me in this endeavor over the past decade come flooding into my mind. I am filled with deep gratitude for each of them and the variety of ways—small and large—that their support sustained my journey in writing this book and enriched the end result.

I am especially grateful for my husband, Mark, who read every chapter with care. His keen ability to recognize sources of vitality in my written stories, and his fruitful search for stories of discovery made this a significantly better book.

I want to thank the thousands of university students I have been honored to teach about change. I have learned a good deal about change from their stories and experience. Their questions about the discovery process have sharpened my thinking, and their enthusiasm about its use has bolstered my confidence to share it more widely.

As well, I am thankful to the many leaders who opened their organizations for my research. These leaders let me observe daily life and experience their struggles, joys, and hopes with change that inspires a better future. Their stories both richly shape and populate this book.

In addition, I am grateful to the individuals who have read all or parts of this book or its precursors, who have made me aware of valuable content for the book, or who have connected me to critical others who helped facilitate the development of this book. Each of them took time to understand what my work was about and provided me welcome support and resources that improved it. Thank you, my colleagues and friends: Maria Anderson, Michel Anteby, Sue Ashford, Jean Bartunek, David Berry, Shirley Clark, Kathryn Correia, Jane Dutton, Elana Feldman, Martha Feldman, Audrey Holm,

Debbie Kolb, Martha Katz, Marshall Kreuter, Carole Levy, Jina Mao, Barbara Miller-Murphy, Jim O'Connell, Gladys Procyshen, Scott Sonenshein, and Ernesto Ruiz-Tiben.

I also thank the superb professionals who guided me through the writing and publication process. Bill Birchard was an expert writing coach and wizard at helping me sharpen my writing's reach and impact. Lynne Wiklander, a terrific communication coach, helped me see at a deeper level the crucial importance of knowing each particular audience. Early on, Jill Totenberg and Carolyn Monaco, top publishing and marketing experts, shared key knowledge about the publishing world. Allison Wigen, PhD candidate at Boston University, provided outstanding editorial support that made the manuscript submission process seamless.

Finally, I thank three institutional sources of support for my work on this book. My endowed chair at Boston University—the Questrom Professor in Management—provided consistent funding for my work on this book and prior academic articles that laid the foundation for the discovery approach that I develop in this book. Terry Clague and Meredith Norwich of Routledge Books provided important feedback and assistance that extended the reach of this book. The data and charts for the DeltaCare case are being used with the permission of the Academy of Management. They are based on my article in the *Academy of Management Journal*, "Discovery as Abductive Mechanism for Reorienting Habits within Organizational Change." 2020. Vol. 63(6): 1951–1975.

Introduction

How do leaders make the most of new realities that upend beliefs?

Beliefs about leading people. Beliefs about market success. Beliefs about internal processes and practices. Beliefs about stakeholder needs. What happens when those beliefs no longer fit today's realities? When they no longer enable the organization to win as it once did? When you're the one responsible for getting beliefs in line with reality?

At the very least, you're going to feel disoriented. Your gut may churn with discomfort. Your team may doubt your authority. You've got a challenge on your hands. And it requires not just garden-variety change management. It requires reorienting your and everyone else's ill-fitting beliefs to create new ones, and in turn, reorienting your organization's practices to create better futures.

Making that happen—guiding people along the trail to the *ahas* and insights that foster belief change—is what this book is all about. It's about a core practice that's often not recognized—and yet essential—for tackling critical change-management challenges that you have to confront increasingly, and more urgently, with every passing year. In the face of realities that upend prevailing beliefs, you need the skills to get everyone to reimagine, redesign, and rethink the organization.

THE SOLUTION: A PROCESS OF DISCOVERY

Research I've undertaken during my career reveals that, to take advantage of new realities, you need to master a fundamental process

DOI: 10.4324/9781003513681-1

that only a few leaders to date have been championing: the process of discovery. This discovery process fuels *ahas* and insights that support your reorienting of beliefs and creation of novel solutions. It's an ongoing process as well, a process you have to stick with, to foster change in yourself and others that underwrites your better future.

My research shows further that discovery as a process involves much more than people think. It requires going on a journey with others that is powered by three motors. The first motor is surprise; the second, genuine doubt; the third, launching new ways. Using each in turn, and again all iteratively, everyone rises to the challenge of altering ill-fitting beliefs to address those new realities.

It is through these three motors that the discovery process paves the way for people to assess the continued functioning of their core beliefs. Do the beliefs still fit the current situation? Should you let go of prevailing ones and take up new ones? Should you consider, indeed embrace, beliefs you have never before considered? Without engaging all three motors—once, twice, many times—you cannot gain the conviction to let go of the old and put your energy into the new.

Notice that the process of discovery involves not just assigning a few hot shots to assess surprise, wrestle with doubt, consider new ways of working, and then come up with a plan for everyone else to execute to transform the organization. Rather, it involves welcoming, internalizing, and processing the new understanding gained through everyone's engagement with each motor. What do the group's findings and realizations mean—not just to business as usual—but to the core beliefs behind the business?

Think of the three motors as facilitators of belief change. When you, with others, go through surprise, the first motor, you experience a collective waking to the fact of a new reality. *Something isn't right. Why doesn't my current belief work any longer?* A sign of success is when group members are taken aback by what they're recognizing.

When you, with others, walk into the unknown of genuine doubt, the second motor, you start questioning: *Are these beliefs still the best ones to hold?* A sign of success is that you are filled with a sense of *not* knowing. Only your uncertainty—not knowing what to do—will loosen the iron grip of long-held beliefs.

When you and your group launch new ways, the third motor, you enthusiastically search for a new, future way of working. Everyone asks: *What other possibilities might there be?* At this point, you and your group launch action that takes place in the context of implementation. You try on new beliefs and practices that you have assessed as better able to function well in the new reality.

It is only through a discovery process like this that people are inclined to grab the promising handrail of new beliefs as they face up to new realities. And it is only through guiding this process as a leader that you and group members let go of ill-fitting beliefs and take up new ones that propel you, the group, and the organization into the future.

Make no mistake about the centrality of belief change to discovery. In the past, you might have thought of discovery as a natural result in the life of an organization, emerging as if through evolution. Or you might have thought of it as serendipitous, in which happenstance guides you and everyone else to breakthrough innovation, invention, and transformation.

But viewing discovery in this way is incorrect. Although you recognize *that* discoveries are generated, and that they catalyze leaps of progress, you don't get any insight into *how* those discoveries unfold. Worse, you encourage people to step over the process of discovery as if the three motors don't exist. Or even worse yet, you encourage them to sidestep new ideas and perspectives once they do learn how to generate them. And that's a huge loss for everyone.

You're making the mistake of grossly undervaluing and woefully under developing discovery. Despite its game-changing role in work and life, it is getting so little attention that you—and most people—continue to lack the skill to cultivate discovery. The result is that you risk squandering one opportunity after another to reshape your future and that of your organization. As you fail to lead with the three motors of discovery, you forego untold benefits.

The Untapped Power of Discovery aims to inspire and equip you, perhaps for the first time, to incorporate discovery as a process into your work and life. When you and your fellow employees embrace the discovery process, everyone can rise, together, to transform organization-wide beliefs, and in turn meet the challenge of new realities that any type of organization faces at almost every turn.

SELECTING THE STORIES

Anyone who follows the news knows how essential, yet how difficult, such transformation is. The business press is replete with horror stories. Studies suggest that 70 percent of all change initiatives, and 85 percent of cultural change initiatives, fail. That means that only a limited few succeed, of course, and I was intrigued to find stories of organizations and people who had beaten the odds. I wanted to know why this happened, but most especially, I wanted to know *how* they made it happen.

I went on a search for stories of leaders who embraced unexpected, sometimes vague situations in their organizations or communities. I purposely varied my choices of dozens of organizations in my research. I assembled the stories of discovery in large, medium, and small organizations—in hospitality, entertainment, software design, information technology, and other sectors. I have also included stories from a Fortune 200 manufacturing company, health systems in the US and Canada, a US nonprofit, a global, non-governmental collaboration, and more.

When I found them, I also found that in each one, a discovery process that elicited *ahas* about the suitability of beliefs—and in turn how to reshape no longer suitable ones—was the key to success. To be included, each story had to stem from documents from multiple sources. Each one also had to reveal data that provided clues to the use by the organizations' leaders of a discovery process, a process in which leaders, for example, were "taken aback," or "peered into the void of the unknown."

The stories in the book are not always about dramatic transformation. People do not change their organizations into something they are not. They do not become people they're not. Rather, the stories are about people who have created change in their organizations and communities that, through a re-orientation of beliefs, inspired action toward a better future.

OVERVIEW OF THE BOOK

As a leader, your journey on the road to discovery begins when you learn the central role the process of discovery plays to spark and fuel human creativity, both in your own work and across your organization. Your journey continues as you learn to guide people in operating the motors that fuel discovery. It culminates when you and others conduct multiple cycles of discovery and generate multiple insights. That's when you reorient patterns of belief and practice that spur genuine transformation.

In the process, you will gain a new perspective and use new tools to deal with, or even avoid, gut-wrenching periods where you miss insights that would benefit you in mastering new realities. You will learn a brand-new process to move from suppressing to eagerly cultivating *ahas*.

The Untapped Power of Discovery opens by examining how leaders suppress discovery. In chapter 1, you will learn the three main behaviors of leaders who, often without awareness, thwart new realitcmies and derail discovery. The rest of the book presents a plan to develop the personal and organizational skills for cultivating discovery. Chapter 2 portrays leaders of two mature organizations—in the information technology and health sectors—who navigate a discovery process that reorients outdated beliefs and creates new ways of working that sustain success. It also introduces the "discovery cycle" that helps you learn how discovery's core motors and dynamics of belief change are set into motion.

The following three chapters (chapters 3 through 5) describe those core motors and elements of the discovery process approach, providing specific strategies, questions, and tools to enable you to put them into action now. Each chapter builds out the process for generating the *ahas* and insights that spur belief change.

Chapter 3 examines the motor of surprise. It shows how you can use three common enablers to capitalize on this powerful motor for igniting discovery. Chapter 4 examines the motor of genuine doubt. Through greater awareness of doubt's latent value, and through skilled use of three discovery enablers, you learn how to harness doubt as a generative power that fuels insight and new ideas. Chapter 5 examines the third and final motor of discovery, launching new ways. It shows how, once you learn discovery enablers based in situated action, you can turn vague, yet promising new possibilities into new ways of operating.

The final three chapters show how to fortify discovery's generative power. Through a case study of a global collaboration to eradicate Guinea worm disease developed in chapter 6, you will learn how to help people build their capacity for engaging and conducting discovery through the use of three important enablers: building diverse representation, fostering respectful engagement, and enacting flexible roles. In chapter 7, you will learn how to use the multiplier effect of discovery when you sponsor the repeated use of discovery cycles. Through the use of multiple cycles, you and other leaders and employees can generate consecutive insights and *ahas* that spur belief and behavior change for full transformation. The last chapter brings *The Untapped Power of Discovery* to a close with a call to integrate discovery processes into change management for greatest gain (chapter 8).

INVITATION

We are in a moment filled with new realities that upend our beliefs. It can be a daunting moment in which to see and create new possibilities for achieving a different and better future. We feel hopeless in our ability to effect change. Although a desire for a better future is a vital part of our human society, we often disbelieve that our action can make a difference.

Yet this moment is also an opportunity for organizational and community leaders, together with their stakeholders, to build a different kind of capacity—one that enables everyone to reshape their beliefs in the service of creating novel solutions to the challenges of unexpected situations and new realities. This capacity is discovery, a process that significantly elevates other processes, such as traditional change management, design thinking, and innovation.

A mountain of new research—much of it in this book—suggests that when you, *with* your colleagues, make discovery continuous, when you generate one cycle of discovery after another, you will realize escalating transformative impact. As you confront new realities, you will generate new beliefs that foster growth as a community. Everyone will learn how to routinely—reflexively—catalyze the discovery on which you depend. With multiple cycles of discovery, you'll provoke new ideas and possibilities to create change you had not ever believed possible.

This book invites you, as a leader, to imagine people in *all* organizations as able to generate *ahas* and insights that open new possibilities and perspectives. These, in turn, promote change in beliefs and practices that inspire a better future—often against unbelievable odds, for themselves and others. As a leader you can shed top-down interventions and directives for a more nuanced and expansive approach to change: one that engages people rather than controls them; one that actively explores what is *not known*, rather than rigidly adhering to what is already known; and one that delivers a dynamic organization that thrives as it faces the challenge of each new reality in today's flood of change.

In the process, you will learn to make the discovery of insight, new perspectives, and new possibilities more dependable and systematic. With this discovery repertoire, you will embolden your team and organization to move away from know-it-all ways of operating and on to emerging ones that will enable you and others to master the nebulous new realities and unexpected situations that upend beliefs.

~~~~~

1. Identify a new reality or unexpected situation that upended your beliefs. Which of your beliefs were upended? How did you respond?
2. What ideas in this introduction catch your attention? Why?

# Suppressing Discovery

In his role as engineer and borehole driller, Ronnie Stuyver had traveled throughout Africa. He had the chance to enjoy the children in villages who would gather around him, fascinated with his work. He also observed firsthand the difficulties villagers faced in getting clean water, and that experience prompted him to come up with a new idea to replace traditional hand pumps that served local wells.

Stuyver's idea was simple but insightful in the way it combined elements of what he had observed in villages. He would install a merry-go-round pumping device connected to the wellhead. When children spun the merry-go-round, they would pump water into an elevated storage tank. The villagers could then get gravity-fed clean water on demand. Stuyver was doing what many entrepreneurs do. Perceiving an important, unmet need, he took dissimilar ideas and combined them in a way to create something new.[1]

Stuyver displayed his new device at the 1989 agricultural fair in Pretoria, South Africa. That's where he met Trevor Field, an advertising executive who was wandering the fairgrounds. Field, viewing the prototype, remembered having recently seen women in a rural village standing beside a wind-powered pump waiting for the wind to blow so they could access water. With this new technology, no longer would the women have to endure such hardships. The merry-go-round pump could become the best solution to alleviate the water crisis in Africa.[2]

Field and Stuyver, encouraged by other people's enthusiasm for the idea,[3] decided to work together on a larger version of the prototype. They also brainstormed improvements. For example, an earlier version

DOI: 10.4324/9781003513681-2

of the merry-go-round turned in only one direction. They changed the design to have it move in both directions, after children said they wanted that. Thus was born an invention with terrific promise.

Field and two business colleagues licensed the PlayPump water system from Stuyver in 1994. As continuing champions of the effort, Field believed they had the perfect solution to a deeply concerning situation. He and his colleagues placed all bets on this promising discovery. But what they failed to see—and what leaders of organizations large and small often fail to see—was that their sustained success would stem not just from this initial act of discovery. It would come from a continual discovery process that would enable them to generate insight and reorient beliefs and practices that no longer fit emerging challenges. Without sustaining discovery, they would stop momentum and suppress insights critical to the success of their project.

After installing the first two systems in South Africa's Masinga District, in 1997 Field founded Roundabout Outdoors, a for-profit organization to develop, install, and maintain the systems. PlayPump appeared poised to be a success and a remarkable advance for many water-deprived villages.

Two events contributed to PlayPump's early good fortune. In 1999, South African President Nelson Mandela not only visited a school where a PlayPump had been installed, but he also spun on it along with some of the children.[4] That action triggered a burst of positive press. The following year, Roundabout Out-doors received the acclaimed World Bank Development Marketplace Award,[5] an annual competitive program that funds innovative, early-stage development projects. That success brought more laudatory press. Roundabout Outdoors used the grant of $165,000 to install 40 PlayPumps in South African villages.

Showing great promise, the new technology captured the imagination of philanthropists, who underwrote the venture. In 2004, the Kaiser Family Foundation provided $250,000 to install 60 PlayPumps in South Africa. The South African Department of Water Affairs and Forestry matched the grant to support an additional 60 PlayPumps. In 2005, the *Frontline* show on Public Broadcasting Service aired a video on PlayPump that enhanced its visibility in the United States.[6]

In September 2006, First Lady Laura Bush announced a $60 million public–private partnership between the US government and the nonprofit Case Foundation.[7] It was known as the PlayPump Alliance. "Finding clean drinking water is a central daily task of many women and girls in Africa," the First Lady said.[8] The partnership "will work to provide clean water [for] 10 million people in sub-Sahara Africa by 2010 and support the provision and installation of PlayPump water systems in approximately 650 schools, health centers and HIV-affected communities."[9]

The donors and leaders of Roundabout Outdoors heralded Play-Pump as a new way of accessing clean water. It promised to reduce villagers' struggles with traditional hand pumps.[10] In December 2006, the Case Foundation established PlayPump International-US (PPI), a charitable fundraising and marketing arm for the organization. By early 2008, Roundabout Outdoors had installed 1,000 PlayPumps in South Africa and Mozambique. The target was set at 4,000 Play-Pumps to be installed by 2010, enough to bring clean water to ten million people.

This was a remarkable rollout, but it also lulled Field into thinking that they knew everything they needed to know to achieve the installation target. Field and his team assumed, as in short-lived success stories of similar kinds, that their discovery of a winning idea happens early and once. As a result, they anticipated smooth sailing during implementation, without subsequent surprises or questions that would negatively impact their goals.

But reports of difficulties with PlayPump began to emerge from the field in late 2007. Some pumps had stopped working. Others worked well only in villages with large schools with many children. In villages with few children, the PlayPump water system often went unused because older people didn't spin on the merry-go-round. Women still had to go long distances for water and soon wished for the return of the old hand pumps.

A UNICEF evaluation[11] circulated in October of that year described PlayPump as "an innovative and robust technology" that could be improved readily with modification. However, it also noted that the technology-driven strategy Roundabout Outdoors deployed to install PlayPump systems "required serious and urgent revision." Moreover, their dedication to a strategy of quick scaling overlooked key problem areas, including inadequate community input and poor site location.

Then in April 2008, an independent evaluator for Skat Consulting Ltd. (Swiss Resource Center and Consultancies for Development) completed a technical and social assessment of PlayPump implementation in Mozambique. Like the UNICEF report, the Skat evaluator found inadequate community involvement. The team found "no signs that communities had been consulted prior to installation or had a say in choosing the pump type of their choice."[12]

The UNICEF and Skat reports started to put their finger on the management failing. The leaders and donors believed so much in PlayPump that they didn't doubt their initial "perfect solution"[13] to accessing clean water. The response to the reported failures and difficulties? Leaders at Roundabout Outdoors and PPI seemingly ignored them. They continued to install new pumps, still trying to achieve the goal of 4,000 installed pumps. This marked the juncture when the project began unraveling. Ironically this occurred at a promising moment when the initiative still could have been salvaged.

This surely sounds familiar if you're in an organization that has stumbled during the rollout of new products, services, processes, and practices. No one stopped to reconsider the organization's direction or investigate the difficulties as they emerged from the field. By staying the course to achieve targets and ignoring clues to difficulties, the leaders suppressed—instead of sustained—ultimate success. They assured that they didn't learn what they didn't know. They didn't pursue discovery.

In late 2009, the Case Foundation admitted that PPI had identified "significant concerns" with maintenance of the installed pumps in specific areas. The initial soaring success was coming to a rough landing. Although the PlayPump technology held much promise and hope, the project ended in 2010, five years after it began.[14]

The effort to install PlayPump failed, but not for lack of money. Nor did it fail because the collaboration of inventor, entrepreneur, and funders wasn't dedicated to solving the challenge of getting clean water to villagers in Africa. The collaborators all believed passionately that clean water was one of the great issues of our time.[15] Addressing the challenge by installing PlayPumps would greatly improve human lives.

So, what went wrong? At the time, official accounts of unused and broken pumps in the field suggested the project failed[16] for two main reasons: inadequate maintenance on installed pumps and location of some pumps in places without adequate supply of quality groundwater. But these reasons, although relevant for understanding the technical failure, provide little insight into why, once installation began, the collaboration couldn't lead to success.

The real reason for the failure of PlayPump is that the leaders and donors made the same mistake that many leaders do. Instead of sustaining discovery, they suppressed it. By taking PlayPump as the perfect—and finished—solution, they failed to see discovery as a process. A process that needed to evolve the project, not just during design, but throughout implementation and beyond. By treating PlayPump as the end of their discovery, they curtailed its power and use as a process. For lack of that discovery process, they failed to fulfill PlayPump's early promise of sustained access to clean water in Africa.

A CONSTRAINED VIEW OF DISCOVERY

Most people conceive of discovery in a very limited way. It is a scientific breakthrough, the latest cutting-edge technology, the new life-saving drug, the novel design. Discovery is then associated with the outcome created. The new entity, the finished product or service that embodies the eureka moment.

But by relegating discovery to an outcome, we relegate it to designers. We presume it is somebody else's job. As a result, we severely curtail the use and power of discovery as part of a process for human growth and positive change. This outcome-oriented view overlooks more of the potential gains from discovery than it reveals.

A persistent error by many leaders today is to completely miss how discovery operates. They miss the critical role of discovery as a mechanism for generating new advances. They miss the wide spectrum of people who can contribute to the process. For example, they fail to recruit people besides designers, technologists, and scientists. With this constrained view of discovery, leaders have only a basic rendering of a bigger horizon that promises significant gains across every organization.

By all evidence, the leaders in the PlayPump collaboration held a constrained view of discovery. They made a common mistake that turns promising initiatives into stunted successes. They believed in the new technology. It was the perfect solution to the issue of clean water for all villages of South Africa and beyond. No adaptation was necessary. Tied to the most constrained view of discovery, they unwittingly undercut their success. A grasp of discovery as an ongoing process would have served them better.

In hindsight, we can point to many missed opportunities. They didn't anticipate the need to search for what they wouldn't know—nobody could know—about an early invention's use in the field. Nor apparently did they anticipate what they would learn about the maintenance issues that surfaced early. Excited, they were hopeful the installation of PlayPump would alleviate much hardship—and it did at first.

This is where so many leaders risk finding themselves. They have reached the moment of highest hopes at the advent of a eureka idea embodied in a product or service. When difficulties start to emerge and collide with the felt urgency to further implement and achieve pre-set goals, no one stops to reconsider how the lack of a discovery process is the root problem. At PlayPump, the collaboration didn't further the process of discovery. Instead, they suppressed it. They stayed the course to reach the goal of 4,000 installed pumps—and dismissed the opportunity to generate insight and new understanding that could have alerted them that course correction was urgently needed.

In organizations today, many leaders, in effect, urge people all the time to halt the discovery process. That's what sets up organization after organization for its next stumble. And that's what set the stage for the PlayPump collaboration's failure. Instead of aiding this process—which a collaboration works well for—they held it back. That encouraged them to rapidly scale up installation as the answer to improving millions of lives. As Trevor Field noted, "when you see people dying of thirst, I don't think research and evaluation is top of my list."

This constrained view also encouraged Field and Stuyver to think of discovery, as most leaders do, as a one-off, discrete event conducted by people with special talent (design experts, scientists). Only these designated people can generate insight and novel ideas. Everyone else lacks the natural creative talent assumed necessary for discovery. This reinforces the outdated thinking of Taylorism,[17] in which some people are viewed as having the "head" for insight and others the "hands" for implementation.

In business organizations, this approach creates the belief that leaders create change and employees carry it out. In universities, it validates the belief that tenured faculty should design new curriculum and lecturer faculty should implement it. In classrooms, it reinforces the belief that teachers know and students should learn from teachers. The expectations associated with this dichotomy—discovery (head) versus implementation (hand)—hamper widespread involvement and shut down discovery.

Huge costs for creativity are incurred when leaders hold a constrained view of discovery. In addition to excluding people from contributing to discovery, they support the perception of the discovery process as mysterious, or serendipitous, occurring solely by chance, or requiring a leap of faith instead of a lot of work. Although people might recognize that they have generated *ahas* and other discoveries, they don't acquire any insight into *how* this happened. This limited sightline, paradoxically, makes most leaders uncomfortable and unwilling to embrace discovery as a process.

The constrained view of discovery might make managing more controllable, at least in the short term. It also fits with leaders' preferred ways of operating. Most leaders don't like surprise, which brings new insight and unpredictability. They prefer predictability. Most leaders are uncomfortable with doubt and questions, which new realities and challenges generate. They prefer the certainty of knowing. And most leaders don't like trying new ways of operating. They prefer planning and execution. As you might suspect, the constrained view of discovery fits leaders like a well-worn glove, precisely because it affirms traditional beliefs about effective management. No surprise, no doubt, and no experimenting.

But all these prevailing beliefs also suppress discovery. This is a tragedy that befalls organization after organization.

DISCOVERY DERAILERS

Even when they claim to support innovation and creativity, people with the best of intentions suppress discovery. For example, an experimental study conducted by Jennifer Mueller, Shimul Melwani, and Jack Goncalo[18] found that when motivated to increase certainty, participants associated novel ideas with uncertainty and failure. They were less likely to recognize creative ideas. They were also receptive only to those ideas that maintained predictability and fit with existing practice. Their false sense of certainty quashed new ideas and possibilities.

Such research points to what I call "discovery derailers." There are three main ones that leaders practice: they ignore unsettling clues; they explain away discrepancies; and they censor contrary ideas. Each derailer creates the illusion of certainty by protecting beliefs from new realities. In a sense, each is a means to reinforce current, outdated beliefs that channel promising initiatives to failure. Each derailer, in other words, heads off discovery before it starts or undermines a discovery process underway.

Ignoring Unsettling Clues

As a discovery derailer, ignoring unsettling clues is quite common. After the fact, people offer familiar sayings that signal the lapse: "We just didn't think about that . . . " "How could we have missed that?" "We didn't see it coming . . . " It is not hard to imagine saying these things ourselves even though the clues to our troubles were there all along.

Clues are critical to perceive because they point to what is not known, or what remains hidden from view. They also suggest that things might not be as they are—or as we think they should be. However, while clues are helpful for recognizing unexpected new realities, facing those realities can be uncomfortable. Consequently, people ignore unsettling clues, preferring instead to deal with information and facts. We stay the course, avoiding uncertainty and affirming current beliefs about how things should operate.

As a discovery derailer, ignoring clues shuts down an organization's search into what is not known or uncomfortable realities. In the case of PlayPump, the collaboration ignored clues that signaled difficulties. A key one was that pumps went unused in those villages with older demographics. The collaboration continued their main work of installing 4,000 pumps by 2010 regardless of what else was happening.

If the clues had been examined—even as uncomfortable and disruptive to production as that might have been—the collaboration could have gained important insight into installation difficulties and how to creatively address them. Instead, the difficulties ultimately led to the end of the project.

This happens to all of us, even scientists who are trained to discover. Professor Sen Chai[19] conducted a study of near misses and ultimate successes in the scientific discovery process of the ribonucleic acid interference (RNAi) gene-silencing phenomenon. In her research, she found that scientists who were on the verge of discovering the new phenomenon nevertheless missed it because they failed to recognize anomalies that didn't fit within the confines of their notion of "normal science." If these scientists had instead considered anomalies as clues in a discovery process, they would have been better positioned to notice the unexpected. Moreover, when other scientists sometimes noticed these clues, they nevertheless ignored them as not pertinent to the present investigation. By not letting go of their long-held beliefs, even temporarily, the scientists ignored the anomalies—evidence that could have helped them see how close they were to the discovery.

As a discovery derailer, ignoring unsettling clues protects people from having their prevailing beliefs challenged, which allows them to keep their attention focused on pre-set plans, goals, or hypotheses—often to their detriment.

Explaining Away Discrepancies

Explaining away discrepancies is another common discovery derailer. More than ignoring clues, this action explicitly minimizes the significance of new ideas and allows people to redouble their grip on prevailing beliefs and practices.

To see how this works, put yourself in the medical shoes of the surgeons at British Royal Infirmary (BRI) in the 1990s. Their institution was designated by the United Kingdom's National Health Service as one of nine regional centers to provide open heart surgery for children.[20] They could take pride that their performance was on par with that of other designated centers. However, while all other centers improved their performance over time, BRI did not.

Over almost a decade, BRI continued to perform pediatric cardiac surgeries despite slipping performance. According to the evidence,[21] from 1990 to 1995, its procedures produced "between 30 and 35 excess deaths over what would have been expected if the unit had been 'typical'" based on other centers' performance. Then, in 1995, the worst happened. A child died during surgery. That prompted a formal review. The conclusion? "Confusion" reigned at BRI.

Observers of the tragic trajectory found it hard to understand. Many people in the public wondered: Why had the surgeons continued to perform pediatric cardiac surgery in the face of dismal performance?

This is when BRI explained away the discrepancies. BRI surgeons and officials believed their substandard performance was due to the severity of cases handled—tougher cases meant tougher results. While that explanation may have made some sense on the surface, as reported in the investigation, it ended up proving invalid. The data showed its falsity in black and white.

So, why hadn't the surgeons and officials probed further? Why did they explain away the discrepancies in performance, even in the face of the deadly result?

BRI surgeons could not bring themselves to use performance data to test the veracity of their own assessment. They didn't think "we are doing something wrong and need to improve." Rather, they thought, we are doing our best with "sicker children."[22] Doubling down on their belief that case severity caused the dangerous complications and deaths, they created a certitude that made their thinking and practice even more rigid. As a result, they quashed the potential to discover what was necessary to improve clinical standards and protect children's safety and lives.

Surgeons are not the only people who explain away discrepancies. Action research conducted by organizational psychologist Chris Argyris showed how management consultants explain away their performance problems. When challenged by less-than-desirable results in projects, the consultants did not question their own performance and expertise. Instead, they blamed clients and managers. For example, said a consultant in one of Argyris' studies, "They [clients and managers] have to be open to change and want to learn."[23]

By explaining away discrepant feedback on results as their customers' faults, the consultants protected their belief in their own expertise. They protected themselves against exploring their performance, discovering new insights, processes, and practices, and from potentially having to adjust to new realities.

Scientists also get into the explain-away business. A case in point: For much of the 1900s, prevailing theory about the human body during exercise held that a lack of oxygen reaching muscles led to lactic acid production. That, in turn, led to muscle burn and fatigue. Coaches guided athletes to work out just below their "lactic threshold." Few people at the time questioned this view. Then, research published by George Brooks—a PhD in exercise physiology and himself a high school track runner—demonstrated that lactic acid was really a source of energy, not a waste product.

Brooks couldn't get much of a hearing for his research. "I had huge fights," he recalled later. "I had terrible trouble getting my grants funded; I had my papers rejected." But over time the accumulating evidence proved him right, and other scientists started to build on his work.[24] This change of heart by other scientists only came after they explained away discrepancies for much longer than one would have thought. They had to stop explaining away the findings discrepant with their beliefs before they could discover new insights from lactic-acid research.

To some people, the trajectory of Brooks' story was not a surprise. In his book *The Structure of Scientific Revolutions*,[25] Thomas Kuhn, a notable philosopher of science, proposed a model of scientific progress consisting of alternating "normal" and "revolutionary" phases. During "normal" periods, scientists adhere to a "paradigm," a pattern of prevailing belief that governs the standards and practice of research. Researchers generate incremental knowledge within dominant theories and methods. Should discrepancies from predominant knowledge occur, researchers try to resolve them within the prevailing paradigm. Or they explain them away as "noise in the data" or methodological artifacts.

"Normal science," writes philosopher Ian Hacking in Kuhn's introduction, "does not aim at novelty but at clearing up the status quo. It tends to discover what it expects to discover."[26] In other words, it doesn't sustain a process of discovery to the extent that scientists would like to think.

Over time, discrepancies nevertheless erode confidence in the paradigm, just as happened with Brooks' research on lactic acid. That's when the "revolutionary" phase begins. Scientists aim to discover what they do not expect to discover by examining contrary evidence and ideas. The former paradigm gets replaced with reoriented beliefs and practices that eventually usher in the next phase of normal science.

Given their extensive training, professionals, including scientists, surgeons, and management consultants, are prone to use this discovery derailer. When faced with evidence discrepant with their belief, the tendency of professionals to behave defensively is well documented.[27] Without concerted effort, any of us can protect prevailing beliefs by explaining away discrepant evidence and suppressing an opportunity for discovery.

Censoring Contrary Ideas

During my observation of a strategic planning meeting of senior leaders in a Fortune 200 company,[28] a new division sales manager recommended an idea to improve future product distribution. Instead of always using their own distributors, he recommended the division sell a particular product through the distributors of a recent acquisition.

The group president asked whether this product would carry their name or the name of the acquired company. The sales manager replied that the product would carry their name due to customer recognition, even though it would be distributed through the acquired company's distributors. The group president, surely with distributor relationships in mind, replied, "uh hum." As he did this, he nodded slightly and lowered his eyelids, no longer looking at the manager.

During a subsequent break, this sales manager told me that he "knew" from the group president's response to his suggestion that he should not pursue the issue any further. He indicated that the group president's concern was "not to get the customary distributors mad" by having a product sold through the acquired company's channels.

SUPPRESSING DISCOVERY 19

Through his behavior, the group president had censored an idea that was contrary to customary practice. Of course, it might have been a bad idea, destined for his veto no matter how he managed the discussion, but his handling of the idea not just revealed his opinion, but also demonstrated his tendency to suppress the discovery process. Like many managers, he shut down discussion of a contrary idea even though it could have opened the discussion. He had succumbed to censoring, and as a result, couldn't reap the potential gain from further discussion.

This situation is not unique. Extensive research suggests that despite best intentions, managers censor contrary ideas. Based on their study of employee voice, which details the way managers censor employee input,[29] organizational researchers James Detert and Ethan Burris[30] caution managers, "Many of your people are more likely to keep mum than to question initiatives or suggest new ideas at work."

For example, managers censor input by sending nonverbal cues that they are in charge, such as crossing their arms in front of others or dressing formally. Likewise, the group president sent the nonverbal cue of lowered eyelids and turning away from the sales manager. These cues make employees reticent to speak. Managers also censor ideas through formal mechanisms. Ironically, this includes even suggestion boxes to solicit anonymous comments. That's because the formality highlights the riskiness of speaking up. People assume that if anonymous vehicles for input are needed, giving input must be risky.

In addition to censoring from the top down, leaders can foster the censoring of contrary ideas that happens from the bottom up. That's when, for example, junior leaders and employees stop themselves from bringing up ideas that go against the organization and senior leaders' grain—input they perceive as risky. They shy away from anticipated pushback and potential sanction. They engage in self-censoring.

Consider a study of how teams and individuals suppress anomalies. Researchers David Snowden, Gary Klein, Chew Lock Pin, and Cheryl Ann Teh tracked how teams composed of either military or intelligence officers reacted to clues that they were mistaken.[31] The research deployed a garden path scenario—a methodology in which the presented scenario leads participants into adopting an incorrect view of what is going on. The researchers wanted to see how long it took the leaders and their team members to discover the real story. Only by taking notice of subtle cues inserted along the way could the officers in the study realize the mistaken view they held.

The teams of military officers received a scenario about a possible invasion, and the teams of intelligence officers received one about a homeland security concern. As expected, the participants interpreted the scenarios with the anticipated storyline to which the garden path initially led them, but the scenarios also featured a set of weak signals that suggested something other than the anticipated plotline was unfolding. These weak signals became stronger over time.

Here was the challenge: To "get off the garden path," the teams needed to notice something going on that was different from what they expected. They needed to discover the real story, and you would think these people would be experts at just that. The results, though, surprised even the researchers. First, nobody on any of the teams ever recognized the real story, even at the end. As Gary Klein, the co-lead on the study remarked, "Each team persisted in believing the original story as if nothing had happened."[32]

However, upon reviewing the digital diaries of individual team members' observations during the study, researchers learned just how tied to the garden path were the participants. Someone on each team—sometimes more than one—wrote about the weak cues in their diary. They had noticed them. Yet, these individuals rarely mentioned the insight to the leader. In the very few instances when they did, their leader ignored it. The full team was never informed.

That was not the end of the story. When Klein presented these findings to a US intelligence agency, several junior analysts spoke up to express their belief that their units acted in exactly the way as described in the experiment. With Klein's prompting, the analysts admitted to all assembled that they had indeed censored themselves, being reluctant to express ideas that were counter to prevailing beliefs. Klein describes the subsequent back and forth between the junior and senior analysts:

> Senior analysts in the room were shocked. They argued that the organization encouraged everyone to give his or her independent views. The junior analysts held firm. What the senior analysts said might be the official position, but it didn't reflect how the organization worked. They didn't want to risk their promotions by making unpopular statements.[33]

More than ignoring clues or explaining away discrepancies, censoring and self-censoring contrary ideas creates a fear-based atmosphere that reinforces rigidity of beliefs. That rigidity suppresses any opportunity for discovery. Indeed, at the root of each discovery derailer is not a lack of vision, time, patience, or effort. Nor is it a blind spot or oversight related to technology or business practices. Rigidly held beliefs stifle insight.[34] These beliefs set people's minds in concrete.

With training, however, discovery derailers are not usually hard to recognize. The key to halting suppression of discovery? Recognize what is happening and treat the derailer as a call to action: It's time to reignite the process of discovery.

TREAT DISCOVERY DERAILERS AS A HELPFUL WAKE-UP CALL

The first step in reigniting discovery is to heed challenges to prevailing beliefs and practice. Then, recognize them as a time to course-correct. That's not to say this process is easy, but sometimes the call to action comes as a wake-up call to ignite a discovery process.

It turns out the leaders of the Case Foundation and PPI heard the wake-up call and recognized they needed to rededicate themselves to the discovery process. In blogs posted in September 2009 and May 2010, CEO and Case Foundation co-founder Jean Case noted publicly how the foundation had to re-think its involvement with PlayPump. She wrote:

> at the Case Foundation we've had to face our own hard moments when reality has set in. Things don't materialize as envisioned, and you fall short of your mark. It's easy to feel discouraged or even embarrassed. You can't help but worry about what people will think, or the price you might pay in the court of public opinion. We experienced this recently, as we had to re-think our involvement in the PlayPump initiative.[35]

The Foundation identified three possible courses of action for the future of PPI. The first was to ignore the unsettling clues as they had been doing, which meant "to stay the course, ignore the emerging realities, and stubbornly continue on a path that the growing evidence was suggesting was unwise." The second possibility was to "pull the plug on the effort and conclude that the time and capital was better invested elsewhere." The final possibility was to "take a step back and regroup," proceeding in a "new and more effective way."[36]

They chose the third option. By doing so, they stopped ignoring the unsettling clues and ignited a discovery process. Said Jean Case,

> Our support of health and humanitarian efforts in Africa has opened our eyes and taught us much about challenges and opportunities. [T]hey've taught us that each country, and indeed each village, in Africa brings its own unique characteristics, making a "one size fits all" solution to entrenched problems unrealistic and posing significant barriers to scale.[37]

The organization still held to its original belief that clean water was one of the most significant issues of our era. That was a belief that genuinely didn't need to change. But they learned—painfully at times—that they could act in more effective ways for everyone's benefit. To do this required altering other core beliefs, notably their belief in PlayPump as the perfect solution for all communities. They realized that PlayPump only worked in specific villages, and they recognized the difficulties with installation. They also loosened their hold on a constrained view of discovery. PlayPump technology—the initial discovery—became the stepping-off place for an *ongoing* process of discovery in which they sought to create a new, more effective way forward.

In May 2009, the PPI board hired a new CEO to regroup and plan for the future. This inquiry led in December 2009 to PPI finalizing an agreement with Water for People, a global nonprofit organization that helps people bring clean water and sanitation solutions on a sustained basis to their local communities. Water for People would become an "implementing partner," receiving the pump inventory and funds to install them. Three months later, in March 2010, PPI announced it would close and transition all assets to this partner.

PlayPump became one solution in a larger portfolio of water solutions offered by Water for People to "meet the safe water needs of specific rural communities."[38] Rural communities could select which solution best met their situation. The blog from Aid Watch,[39] New York University's Development Research Institute, commented at the time:

> This seems like the right outcome. We can ask why it took so long to see the flaws in the PlayPump model. But in contrast to the official aid world, where the old, failed solutions keep getting recycled across 60 years, this is real progress!

The PlayPump initiative moved forward through the school of hard knocks. The leaders learned over almost two decades that enabling, not suppressing discovery, would lead to a more effective way to come up with a successful solution. They, of course, serve just as a case to make the point of this book. Unintentionally, surgeons, consultants, engineers, senior leaders, employees, entrepreneurs, donors, and scientists suppress discovery when faced with unsettling situations that challenge their prevailing beliefs. The discovery derailers protect them from scrutinizing those beliefs and allow them to maintain the status quo and preserve certainty and control. Suppression remains their default option, but it need not remain so.

~~~~~

1. In your organization, is discovery viewed as an outcome or as a process? Do you stay the course or explore the situation when presented with challenges to prevailing beliefs?
2. What discovery derailers have you seen people use? How do they suppress new ideas and insights? Do you fall into the traps of ignoring unsettling clues, explaining away discrepancies, and censoring contrary ideas?
3. How could you and your team treat discovery derailers as a helpful wake-up call? What benefits might that generate?

NOTES

1 Visit this site for a schematic of the new pump that traces the water flow of the new technology: https://news.climate.columbia.edu/2010/07/01/the-playpump-what-went-wrong/
2 March, Elizabeth. 2009 (2nd printing). "When Innovation Is Child's Play." *WIPO Magazine.* www.wipo.int/wipo_magazine/en/2009/02/article_0013.html, accessed June 2023. WIPO stands for the World Intellectual Property Organization.
3 Stellar, Daniel. 2010. "The PlayPump: What Went Wrong? State of the Planet." *Columbia University Climate School.* Blog. https://news.climate.columbia.edu/2010/07/01/the-playpump-what-went-wrong/, accessed June 2023. Stellar noted the enthusiasm for PlayPump.
4 March, Elizabeth. 2009 (2nd printing). "When Innovation Is Child's Play." *WIPO Magazine.* www.wipo.int/wipo_magazine/en/2009/02/article_0013.html, accessed June 2023. This is one of the many sources documenting Mandela's visit.
5 World Bank. 2002. *South Africa: The Roundabout Outdoor PlayPump* (Infobriefs. No. 218). Washington, DC: Africa Region Findings and Good Practice. https:// openknowledge.worldbank.org/handle/10986/9749?locale-attribute=en, accessed June 2023.

6 Costello, Amy. 2005. "South Africa: The PlayPump. Turning Water into Child's Play." *PBS Frontline World*. Video. www.pbs.org/frontlineworld/rough/2005/10/ south_africa_th.html, accessed June 2023.
7 Costello, Amy. 2006. "PlayPump Project Receives Major US Funding." *PBS Frontline World*. Blog. www.pbs.org/frontlineworld/blog/2006/09/playpump_projec.html, accessed June 2023.
8 Ibid.
9 White House Archives. 2006. "Mrs. Bush's Remarks at the Clinton Global Initiative Annual Meeting." https://georgewbush-whitehouse.archives.gov/news/releases/ 2006/09/20060920–4.html, accessed June 2023.
10 Frontline World. 2010. "Troubled Water." Video. www.pbs.org/frontlineworld/stories/southernafrica904/video_index.html, accessed June 2023.
11 UNICEF. 2007. "An Evaluation of the PlayPump® Water System as an Appropriate Technology for Water, Sanitation and Hygiene Programmes." https://www-tc.pbs.org/frontlineworld/stories/southernafrica904/flash/pdf/unicef_pp_report.pdf, accessed June 2023. Despite UNICEF's identification, the report was released prior to vetting and approval by UNICEF.
12 Obiols, Ana Lucia, & Karl Erpf. 2008. "Mission Report on the Evaluation of the PlayPump installed in Mozambique." https://www-tc.pbs.org/frontlineworld/stories/ southernafrica904/flash/pdf/mozambique_report.pdf, accessed June 2023.
13 For example, Steve Case, co-founder of the Case Foundation, called the idea of PlayPumps "simple, but so perfect." Source: Frontline World. 2010. "Troubled Water." Video. www.pbs.org/frontlineworld/stories/southernafrica904/video_index.html, accessed June 2023.
14 Unite for Sight. n.d. "Outcomes are Essential in Global Health, Case Study: PlayPumps." Blog. https://ghu.uniteforsight.org/monitoring-and-evaluationcourse1-outcomes-are-essential, accessed October 2023.
15 Case, Jean. 2010. "The Painful Acknowledgement of Coming Up Short." *Case Foundation*. Blog. https://casefoundation.org/blog/painful-acknowledgment-coming-short/, accessed June 2023.
16 Stellar, Daniel. 2010. "The PlayPump: What Went Wrong? State of the Planet." *Columbia University Climate School*. Blog. https://news.climate.columbia.edu/2010/07/01/the-playpump-what-went-wrong/, accessed June 2023.
17 In 1909, Frederick W. Taylor published "The Principles of Scientific Management." The fourth principle, relevant here, is to "properly divide the workload between managers and workers." Managers should plan the work and train workers to do it. Workers should implement what they have been trained to do.
18 Mueller, Jennifer S., Shimul Melwani, & Jack A. Goncalo. 2011. "The Bias Against Creativity: Why People Desire but Reject Creative Ideas." *Psychological Science* 23(1):13–17.
19 Chai, Sen. 2017. "Near Misses in the Breakthrough Discovery Process." *Organization Science* 28(3):411–428.
20 The British Royal Infirmary example is adapted from: Weick, Karl E., & Kathleen M. Sutcliffe. 2003. "Hospitals as Cultures of Entrapment: A Re-Analysis of the Bristol Royal Infirmary." *California Manage-*

ment Review 45(2):73–84. And from: Weick, Karl E., & Kathleen M. Sutcliffe. 2015. *Managing the Unexpected*, 3rd ed. San Francisco, CA: Jossey-Bass, a Wiley Company.
21 Weick, Karl E., & Kathleen M. Sutcliffe. 2003. "Hospitals as Cultures of Entrapment: A Re-Analysis of the Bristol Royal Infirmary." *California Management Review* 45(2):76.
22 Ibid., 73–84. Citation taken from *Learning from Bristol*. 2002. Crown, page 266.
23 Argyris, Chris. 1991. "Teaching Smart People How to Learn." *Harvard Business Review*, May–June:99–109; Wolfberg, Adrian. 2022. *In Pursuit of Insight: The Everyday Work of Intelligence Agents*. Washington, D.C: National Intelligence University, p. 50.
24 Kolata, Gina. 2006 (May 16). "Lactic Acid Is Not Muscles' Foe, It's Fuel." *New York Times*. www.nytimes.com/2006/05/16/health/nutrition/16run.html, accessed June 2023.
25 Kuhn, Thomas S. 2012. *The Structure of Scientific Revolutions*, 50th Anniversary edition, 4th ed. Chicago and London: The University of Chicago Press.
26 Hacking, I. 2012. "Introductory Essay." In *The Structure of Scientific Revolutions*, 50th Anniversary edition, 4th ed. Edited by Thomas S. Kuhn. Chicago and London: The University of Chicago Press.
27 Argyris, Chris. 1991. "Teaching Smart People How to Learn." *Harvard Business Review*, May–June:99–109; Wolfberg, Adrian. 2022. *In Pursuit of Insight: The Everyday Work of Intelligence Agents*. Washington, D.C: National Intelligence University, p. 50.
28 Golden-Biddle, Karen. 1992. "The Individual and Organizational Culture: Strategies for Action in Highly Ordered Contexts." *Journal of Management Studies* 29:1–21.
29 Detert, James R., & Ethan R. Burris. 2007. "Leadership Behavior and Employee Voice: Is the Door Really Open?" *Academy of Management Journal* 50(4):869–884. See also: Detert, James R., & Ethan R. Burris. 2015 (December 11). "Nonverbal Cues Get Employees to Open Up—or Shut Down." Digital Article. https://hbr.org/2015/12/nonverbal-cues-get-employees-to-open-upor-shut-down-2#:%7E:text=Signal%20%E2%80%9CI%E2%80%99m%20really%20lis, accessed April 2024
30 Detert, James R., & Ethan R. Burris. 2016. "Can Your Employees Really Speak Freely?" *Harvard Business Review*, January–February:1–9.
31 Excerpt adapted from Klein, Gary. 2013. *Seeing What Others Don't*. New York: Public Affairs, pp. 164–166.
32 Ibid., 165.
33 Ibid., 166.
34 I use "rigidity of belief" to capture tightly held beliefs.
35 Case, Jean. 2010. "The Painful Acknowledgement of Coming Up Short." *Case Foundation*. Blog. https://casefoundation.org/blog/painful-acknowledgment-comingshort/, accessed June 2023.
36 Ibid.
37 Case, Jean. 2009. "Autumn Updates from Jean Case." *Case Foundation*. Blog. https:// casefoundation.org/blog/autumn-updates-jean-case/, accessed June 2023.
38 Case, Jean. 2010. "The Painful Acknowledgement of Coming Up Short." *Case Foundation*. Blog. https://casefoundation.org/blog/painful-acknowledgment-coming-short/, accessed June 2023.

39 Freschi, Laura. 2010. "Some NGOs CAN Adjust to Failure: The PlayPumps Story." *AidWatch*. Blog. www.nyudri.org/aidwatcharchive/2010/02/some-ngos-can-adjustto-failure-the-playpumps-story, accessed June 2023.

REFERENCES

Argyris, Chris. 1991. "Teaching Smart People How to Learn." *Harvard Business Review*, May-June:99–109.

Case, Jean. 2009. "Autumn Updates from Jean Case." *Case Foundation*. Blog. https:// casefoundation.org/blog/autumn-updates-jean-case/, accessed June 2023.

Case, Jean. 2010. "The Painful Acknowledgement of Coming Up Short." *Case Foundation*. Blog. https://casefoundation.org/blog/painful-acknowledgment-coming-short/, accessed June 2023.

Chai, Sen. 2017. "Near Misses in the Breakthrough Discovery Process." *Organization Science* 28(3):411–428.

Costello, Amy. 2005. "South Africa: The PlayPump. Turning Water into Child's Play." *PBS Frontline World*. Video. www.pbs.org/frontlineworld/rough/2005/10/south_africa_ th.html, accessed June 2023.

Costello, Amy. 2006. "PlayPump Project Receives Major US Funding." *PBS Frontline World*. Blog. www.pbs.org/frontlineworld/blog/2006/09/playpump_projec.html, accessed June 2023.

Detert, James R., & Ethan R. Burris. 2007. "Leadership Behavior and Employee Voice: Is the Door Really Open?" *Academy of Management Journal* 50(4):869–884.

Detert, James R., & Ethan R. Burris. 2015 (December 11). "Nonverbal Cues Get Employees to Open Up—or Shut Down." Digital Article. https:// hbr.org/2015/12/nonverbal-cues-get-employees-to-open-upor-shut-down-2#:%7E:text=Signal%20%E2%80%9CI%E2%80%99m%20really%20lis, accessed April 2024

Detert, James R., & Ethan R. Burris. 2016. "Can Your Employees Really Speak Freely?" *Harvard Business Review*, January–February:1–9.

Freschi, Laura. 2010. "Some NGOs CAN Adjust to Failure: The PlayPumps Story." *AidWatch*. Blog. www.nyudri.org/aidwatcharchive/2010/02/some-ngos-can-adjust-to-failure-the-playpumps-story, accessed June 2023.

Frontline World. 2010. "Troubled Water." Video. www.pbs.org/frontlineworld/stories/ southernafrica904/video_index.html, accessed June 2023.

Golden-Biddle, Karen. 1992. "The Individual and Organizational Culture: Strategies for Action in Highly Ordered Contexts." *Journal of Management Studies* 29:1–21.

Hacking, I. 2012. "Introductory Essay." In *The Structure of Scientific Revolutions*, 50th Anniversary edition, 4th ed. Edited by Thomas S. Kuhn. Chicago and London: The University of Chicago Press.

Klein, Gary. 2013. *Seeing What Others Don't*. New York: Public Affairs.

Kolata, Gina. 2006 (May 16). "Lactic Acid Is Not Muscles' Foe, It's Fuel." *New York Times*. www.nytimes.com/2006/05/16/health/nutrition/16run.html, accessed June 2023.

Kuhn, Thomas S. 2012. *The Structure of Scientific Revolutions*, 50th Anniversary edition, 4th ed. Chicago and London: The University of Chicago Press.

March, Elizabeth. 2009 (2nd printing). "When Innovation is Child's Play." *WIPO Magazine*. www.wipo.int/wipo_magazine/en/2009/02/article_0013.html, accessed June 2023.

Mueller, Jennifer S., Shimul Melwani, & Jack A. Goncalo. 2011. "The Bias Against Creativity: Why People Desire But Reject Creative Ideas." *Psychological Science* 23(1):13–17.

Obiols, Ana Lucia, & Karl Erpf. 2008. "Mission Report on the Evaluation of the PlayPump Installed in Mozambique." https://www-tc.pbs.org/frontlineworld/stories/ southernafrica904/flash/pdf/mozambique_report.pdf, accessed June 2023.

Stellar, Daniel. 2010. "The PlayPump: What Went Wrong? State of the Planet." *Columbia University Climate School*. Blog. https://news.climate.columbia.edu/2010/07/01/the-playpump-what-went-wrong/, accessed June 2023.

UNICEF. 2007. "An Evaluation of the PlayPump® Water System as an Appropriate Technology for Water, Sanitation and Hygiene Programmes." https://www-tc.pbs. org/frontlineworld/stories/southernafrica904/flash/pdf/unicef_pp_report.pdf, accessed June 2023.

Unite for Sight. n.d. "Outcomes Are Essential in Global Health, Case Study: PlayPumps." Blog. https://uniteforsight.org/global-health-university/outcomes, accessed June 2023.

Weick, Karl E., & Kathleen M. Sutcliffe. 2003. "Hospitals as Cultures of Entrapment: A Re-Analysis of the Bristol Royal Infirmary." *California Management Review* 45(2):73–84.

Weick, Karl E., & Kathleen M. Sutcliffe. 2015. *Managing the Unexpected*, 3rd ed. San Francisco, CA: Jossey-Bass, a Wiley Company.

White House Archives. 2006. "Mrs. Bush's Remarks at the Clinton Global Initiative Annual Meeting." https://georgewbush-whitehouse.archives.gov/news/releases/2006/09/ 20060920-4.html, accessed June 2023.

Wolfberg, Adrian. 2022. *In Pursuit of Insight: The Everyday Work of Intelligence Agents*. Washington, DC: National Intelligence University.

World Bank. 2002. *South Africa: The Roundabout Outdoor PlayPump* (Infobriefs No. 218). Washington, DC: Africa Region Findings and Good Practice. https://openknowledge. worldbank.org/handle/10986/9749?locale-attribute=en, accessed June 2023.

Discovery as a Process

During an interview with *The New York Times* in 2014,[1] shortly after becoming Microsoft CEO, Satya Nadella explained the key challenge for the organization. "Culturally," he said, "I think we have operated as if we had the formula figured out, and it was all about optimizing, in its various constituent parts, the formula. Now it is about discovering the new formula."

Discovering, no longer optimizing, the new formula. That's what discovery as a process is all about. By incorporating this process into their work to create something new, organizations like Microsoft propel themselves to continuing success. Had PlayPump pioneers adopted the same approach, they would have treated their new product to access clean water as only a starting point. They would have built on their initial success, benefiting from one insight after another.

Research I've undertaken for many years reveals that creating new ways in every organization relies on a fundamental process that Nadella has been championing: a process of discovery. In the face of new realities, it paves the way for people to let go of beliefs that no longer guide successful behavior and embrace new ones that do.

By embracing this process together, everyone can meet the critical challenge that organizations and communities face at almost every turn. *How do you make the most of new realities that upend your beliefs?*

The cases of many organizations have shown that the answer depends on this process of discovery. Only when people learn to embrace discovery with that process do they create new ways of working that deliver extraordinary results. That's what Nadella did

DOI: 10.4324/9781003513681-3

in leading people at Microsoft. He used a discovery process to prompt a change in the beliefs of himself, his senior team, and other leaders. He then encouraged the same among employees, and that bolstered the continuous innovation on which Microsoft's success depends.

Nadella urged employees and executives alike to shed current beliefs based on fear. For too long, people believed they had to put individual performance over customer satisfaction. They believed they had to put moving up the ladder over moving forward with innovation. They believed they had to put competing internally on par with competing externally.

Those beliefs, which didn't fit the reality of new competition, hurt, not helped, Microsoft innovate and compete. Nadella explained:

> So, the question is: How do we take the intellectual capital of 130,000 people[2] and innovate where none of the category definitions of the past will matter? Any organizational structure you have today is irrelevant because no competition or innovation is going to respect those boundaries. So how do you create that self-organizing capability to drive innovation and be focused?
>
> To me, that is perhaps the big culture change—recognizing innovation and fostering its growth. It's not going to come because of an org chart or the organizational boundaries. I think what people have to own is an innovation agenda, and everything is shared in terms of the implementation.[3]

Discovering the new formula didn't require an overhaul of organizational structure. It required cultural change generated through a process of discovery. A process that would first help everyone let go of beliefs that drove formula optimization as a goal, and second, help people take on new beliefs that drove the continuous generation of new ideas and products. That was an earthshaking shift, just the shift that many organizations today need to make. It allowed Microsoft to back away from an old focus on winning and toward a new focus on learning. Nadella, in his words, encouraged people to let go of the old beliefs comprising a "know-it-all" culture and adopt a belief in a "growth mindset," a concept developed by Carol Dweck.[4] That meant people would take up the beliefs "that everyone can grow and develop; potential is nurtured, not predetermined; and anyone can change their mindset."[5] The new formula would depend on a "learn-it-all" culture to deliver the continuous stream of discoveries that would stimulate the innovation agenda Nadella was seeking.

Creating a learn-it-all culture is a goal many organizations could benefit from. It assures that the discovery process never ceases. Innovation never ceases. This change at Microsoft generated valuable corollary beliefs: People everywhere in the company should learn new things. They should obsess about customers. They should listen to and encourage colleagues to speak up.[6] These beliefs together would provide the only durable means to deal with the new realities of the market.

In 2019, Microsoft's leaders instituted a management framework to help instill the learn-it-all culture. Joe Whittinghill, corporate vice president of talent, learning, and insights at Microsoft, explains: "Everybody rolled up their sleeves together and came up with our revised definition of the role of managers at Microsoft. It is to deliver success through empowerment and accountability by modeling, coaching, and caring."[7]

Modeling, coaching, and caring became three prized management skills. Leaders began to teach and advocate them to support every manager's role in the learn-it-all culture.[8] Modeling meant living the culture and practicing the growth mindset through example. Coaching meant creating a safe space for employees to grow and learn from mistakes. Caring meant having an expectation and responsibility to be committed to the growth of others.

During the pandemic, leaders leaned on these new beliefs to guide human resources policy and practice. Said Kathleen Hogan, Microsoft executive vice president and chief people officer[9]: It was "less about Covid creating the culture" and more about using Covid to "accelerate" the culture.[10] For example, leaders changed taken for-granted recruiting practices to become more inclusive, screening *in* candidates rather than screening them *out*.

When Nadella assumed the role of CEO in 2014, people wondered whether Microsoft would "make it to the other side."[11] Since then, its learn-it-all culture has spurred growth and innovation. As of June 2, 2023, its market capitalization was $2.49 trillion, versus $318 billion when Nadella took over.[12] That's the kind of difference a process of discovery can make at many companies.

In reflecting on the momentum of this idea, Nadella stressed just how much the generation of beliefs to support the "new formula" had to be an ongoing process across the organization.[13]

> I don't think this would have worked if it was considered new dogma from a new CEO . . . it would have gotten rejected. I think the reason why it has picked up steam and is grounded is twofold:

One is, we framed it, not as a one-time transformation, but as a continuous process of renewal . . . that's helped because we never sort of claimed victory. . . .

The second thing, though, is that I think [our new belief in the growth mindset] speaks to us as human beings. It makes us better parents. It makes us better co-workers. It makes us better leaders. So, it speaks to what I think all of us seek in life and that's the reason why cultural transformation, at least at Microsoft, seems to be working.

Nadella's focus on belief change—letting go of beliefs that no longer fit new realities and taking up new ones that do—remains a critical factor in sustaining Microsoft's leadership in innovation. It shows how even a mature firm, when burdened by beliefs upended by new realities, must rely on a discovery process to sustain success.

REORIENTING BELIEF THROUGH A PROCESS OF DISCOVERY

Beliefs sound like an easy-to-refashion element of organizational culture. If you're a leader, you might wonder why you can't convince people to shed ill-fitting beliefs, like shedding old clothes. What's so hard about adopting new beliefs that better suit the organization's needs, especially when it is under pressure? The explanation for the difficulty comes from the branch of philosophy occupied by pragmatists, who consider beliefs as "habits of expectation." A single action or behavior doesn't count as a belief. It is the "single ways"[14] of many actions and behaviors built through reflection on experience that do.

These habits of expectation dispose us to think and act in certain ways in certain situations.[15] They are "the *way* we do things around here." They are our compass. They guide our trajectory of action. They put us on an easygoing autopilot.

The danger comes when habits of expectation develop that stifle insight and novel ideas. The organization ends up frozen by *rigidity of belief*. Certain ways of thinking and acting harden into propensities to avoid uncertainty. They defeat discovery. When people act, they take their cue from an old compass bearing, regardless of what's happening. What they know to be true because they expect it to be true—their beliefs—prevents them from discovering what they don't know. That's when people succumb to the three derailers of discovery: ignoring, explaining away, and censoring new realities. People become prisoners to their expectations.

By contrast, other habits of expectation foster insight and new ideas, as in Microsoft. They spur *flexibility of belief*, certain ways of acting and thinking that catalyze discovery. People loosen their hold on beliefs that have mired them in the past and embrace new ones to create a more productive future. They explore unexpected realities as opportunities for growth and development. They seek a balance between embracing what they know to be true and what they don't know.

The good news is that since beliefs are dispositional, you can alter them. They can be transformed, adapted, abandoned, or reinvented. When they are in flux, you can search and try new ways to recreate unsettled situations. As a part of a continuous process of discovery, you can undertake cycles of reorienting patterns of belief—away from old ones and toward the new. That continual movement, as my research shows, underpins discovery of all kinds, in both work and life.

This cycle is the centerpiece of the discovery process. It is the single most important mechanism for bringing anything new into the world—whether during innovation, new product development, or organizational change and transformation, large or small. The cycle sounds straightforward, but the flexibility of belief that fuels this cycle requires, as in Microsoft, cultivating a "great readiness."[16] With readiness, you can release patterns of belief that no longer function to guide action in the face of new realities and can embrace reoriented ones that do.

How to create this great readiness is not at all self-evident when we are beset by new realities that challenge beliefs. Letting go of past beliefs is strenuous. Just when we think we have properly loosened our hold on an unfunctional belief—like the pre-pandemic belief that all employees need to come into the office full time for work—we get concerned with the downside. Won't productivity decline when employees are out of sight?

We shy from that struggle. Overcoming our reluctance then becomes a key challenge in cultivating discovery. Even when we know better, we redouble our hold on old beliefs again and again. We push for employees to return to the office—a push that stems from our embrace of belief, not only through intellect but also feelings.[17] We dislike being surprised with unexpected new realities. Our feelings of uncertainty over what will happen if we reorient old beliefs waylay our progress to a surer future.

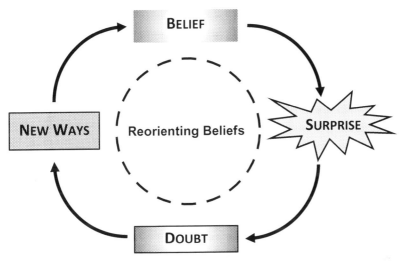

FIGURE 2.1 The basic cycle of discovery.

DISCOVERING NEW WAYS OF DELIVERING CARE

How as a leader do you ignite and keep the discovery process going to create new ways of operating based on reoriented beliefs? The story of DeltaCare,[18] a medium-sized health system, illustrates the approach that integrates discovery into an organization. DeltaCare used a discovery process to transform itself into a health system with an innovative model of healthcare delivery. Its experience highlights what it takes to move away from past patterns of belief and move toward new ones.

Moving Away From Past Patterns of Belief

When Kathryn Correia took over as hospital system president of DeltaCare,[19] she faced the challenge of many hospital CEOs: How to create future value that is essential for sustained survival and growth. When she started inquiring into the system, Correia noticed that it "seemed more like a collection of many things—radiology, lab, outpatient surgery, respiratory therapy—each in their own separate cluster." This made it difficult to understand what the organization needed to do better than anybody else. The situation was nebulous.

Correia took a first step toward encouraging flexibility of belief. She engaged many clinical leaders and managers in conversations and cross-specialty meetings. "What," she asked them, "do we believe will keep DeltaCare in business when patients can go elsewhere? What is the most important thing we do to contribute to care, versus the many things that we do?"

Through her meetings and conversations, she heard many concerns that started to confirm the need for change. For example, she learned that, a year earlier, nurses tried to get hospital leadership to rethink some procedures. The nurses spent too much time running for supplies and hunting down physicians rather than caring for patients. With Correia as the new president, they hoped to address their concerns. Explained one nurse manager: "It was the undying passion of people like us [saying], 'We've got to do something about patient care . . . '" that sparked their outspokenness.

Mapping Care Flows

Correia modeled how a leader can use discovery to drive change. She relied on a lean methodology recently introduced into DeltaCare. Sponsoring a four-day, external consultant–led event,[20] she wanted people "to figure out the hospital" at the highest levels of patient care. To assure broad experience with care delivery, Correia invited a multi-stakeholder group to the event. The group included frontline clinical staff, managers, senior leaders, all of whom were offline for the event's duration.[21] The group also included board members, volunteers, and patients. The patients came from physician referral, self-nomination of volunteers who were also patients, and invitations sent to patients who had written complaints about their care.

Correia advocated early reflection on taken-for-granted beliefs about care delivery. This ignited inquiry into the hospital system, a process grounded in conversations with staff and her observation of potentially problematic service clusters. By continuing the process with broad representation, everyone could reflect on the nebulous situation and, together, get to know it in a deeper way.[22]

Going into this process, Correia and the group members expected to learn that they were mostly delivering care consistent with their current beliefs, which presumed they acted in an integrated and patient-focused manner ("original belief" in Figure 2.2). Even nurses who had prior concerns about care delivery anticipated they would quickly identify issues and blockages that could be addressed to improve care for patients.

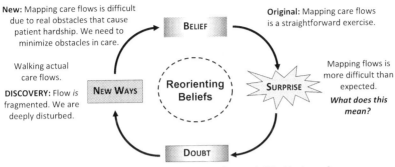

FIGURE 2.2 Creating new ways of delivering patient care.

The group began by mapping flows within and across the highest levels of care delivery: inpatient, outpatient, and emergency. The consultant divided participants into groups according to area, assigning each to smaller rooms to complete this task. Using paper posted on the walls, each group went to work, drawing the flows in their assigned care area to the best of their ability. They identified points of connection, handoffs in flows with the other areas. When connections overlapped areas, group members visited other rooms to gain perspective on their mapping.

The mapping exercise became a core means to drive the organization's early process of discovery, but the mapping offered few rewards at first. Reconvening, all three groups expressed frustration at not being able to map their care processes, even at the highest levels. Instead of coming up with integrated flowcharts, their maps looked more like unfinished puzzles with dead ends and stray pieces. They found it difficult to sort out the various parts that made up patient flows. The project manager recounted the difficulties:

> This mapping exercise is at a very high level, at the 60,000 foot view. And you could *still* see the fragmentation of care . . . the poor handoffs. You could see all the breaking points where there was no integration between patients coming from an ambulatory care into the acute care setting, and back to the ambulatory care.

Seeing the fragmentation disturbed the group members. They hadn't anticipated struggling with mapping the work they engaged in every day ("surprise" in Figure 2.2). They couldn't do what they had set out to do—figure out the hospital system. Everyone realized the mapping should have been a snap. They should have been able to do it with their eyes closed. It had never occurred to them, until they launched into this discovery process, that they couldn't trace the flows of the integrated care they thought they were delivering. They *didn't know* as much as they thought.

This is what happens in many organizations. People in the throes of discovery often feel initially at a loss for how to make sense of an unexpected and discomforting experience. Yet, this discomfort is a positive signal because it means that discovery is at work. The process then turns out to reveal far more that people don't know about the situation than they had anticipated. At DeltaCare, the difficulty with mapping—with its potential of real fragmented care delivery—was the initial big reveal that led to shaking people's confidence in their current beliefs.

You might think there is a way around a breakdown of this kind when you lead or engage in a discovery process. Somehow, if only you were prescient enough, you could figure out a way to dodge the discomfort entirely. Yet, the breakdown of faith in old beliefs proves to be a valuable signal of progress in the process, even though people feel thwarted at the time. The discomfort simply represents a mismatch between the new beliefs and practices needed to rise to the unexpected new reality and the prevailing ones that might have fit the old reality. The situation takes on a diffusely problematic quality. What does the mapping difficulty mean?

At this point in the process at DeltaCare, group members were bumping up against a common wall in the use of discovery. The principles and practices they believed in for providing care couldn't help them get out of this mess. Their current beliefs about how to best deliver care didn't work to guide them in smoothing out their careflow maps. Like most people during a discovery process, they were shocked and taken aback at not being able to continue with their current ways.

You can see how easily leaders in some organizations can miss the chance for genuine discovery at this point. Frustrated, people can explain away the difficulties and potential mismatches as a procedural flaw of the exercise, which can prompt them to stick with the status quo and reassert that they're right. They can also take flowcharts like those at DeltaCare and confine improvements to their own area, redesigning the organization to eliminate only in-group obstacles. They can even put off the issue by delegating it to staff to examine and resolve, perhaps by searching the literature to get an idea of what works elsewhere that can be implemented as best practice.

If Correia and the group members had taken any of these actions at this juncture, they would have derailed the discovery process. Instead, by acknowledging their frustration and the uncertainty, the group kept alive the possibility of benefitting further from grappling with the now unsettled and diffusely problematic situation. Although still not sure what was going on, they sensed the mapping might point to real issues that could lead them to a means for better delivery.

To DeltaCare's credit, sticking with the process of discovery at this point is where they made the choice to sustain discovery and succeed in transforming their delivery system. They asked themselves the blunt but critical questions ("doubt" in Figure 2.2): Could their beliefs about delivering integrated care be wrong? Could some parts of their delivery system be outdated? Could they even be responsible for some of the fragmentation? By not presuming to know what the mapping difficulty meant, the group members steered away from doubling down with rigidity of belief.

That's when DeltaCare set itself apart from many organizations. The group avoided the temptation to suppress discovery. To be sure, they could not avoid running headlong into the wall of a new reality, stunned by their initial inability to get beyond it. But like leaders and employees in other organizations, they understood that with further discovery, their *inability* to make sense of the unexpected difficulty might give way to an *ability* to make *new* sense of it. That's what would lead to new ideas that would successfully resolve the problematic situation.

Moving Toward New Patterns of Belief

Sensing that the process of discovery was leading to answers, the group decided to conduct further inquiry into their nebulous situation by walking the actual patient care flows ("new ways" in Figure 2.2). They hoped that would give them a deeper understanding of patients' actual experience of care. They kept this process informal to put patients at ease. The clinicians put away their white coats, stethoscopes, and beepers. The executives removed their suit jackets. As they then walked with patients, they asked them to describe what was going on for them. They also attended closely to their behavior.

They wanted to examine the factors that contributed to fragmentation without their roles becoming an obstacle.

Walking Actual Care Flows

The group divided into two smaller groups, one of them for inpatient flows and the other for outpatient. They either walked the care flows observing real patients or followed the flow for a typical patient while guided by frontline staff. In short order, the inpatient group discovered how "chaotic" it could be for a hospitalized patient to get services. In one case, only when the transport arrived at the room of a patient scheduled for physical therapy was the transport made aware that the patient was in the radiology department waiting to get an MRI.

Meanwhile, nurses were performing end runs around obstacles to get necessary but delayed services for patients, including blood draws blocked by scheduling bureaucracy or prescriptions for antibiotics held up by late lab results. Summing up the inpatient group walk, a clinical leader noted: "After having problems mapping the flow . . . and watching the difficulties of nurses in progressing patient care, we realized just how often patient care involved heroics."

The outpatient group was likewise surprised. Care delivery was "really not a very patient-friendly experience at all," said one clinician. Patients sent from a specialist's office for diagnostic tests had to negotiate seemingly endless buildings and hospital corridors. Without a previous appointment, they frequently experienced delays, sometimes for hours. Once back at the specialist's office, they often had to make a return trip to the lab for yet more tests. Owing to such hassles, some people preferred to come back on another day.

None of the group members had noticed before how difficult the route through the system was for many patients, nor how especially arduous it was for the elderly and the ill. Said one clinician: "When you walked this flow as a patient, you understood that if you were bringing elderly or very ill people into the hospital, then they were walking way too much for their abilities to get their testing done."

Reconvening after walking the care flows, group members described their experiences as "eye-opening," "discomforting," and "very revealing." The clinicians realized that although they knew patient flows within their own treatment areas, they had little knowledge of the flows between patient admission and discharge. Overall, they expressed chagrin at having observed so many "patient struggles," especially for the most vulnerable patients.

Said Maria Rodgers (chief nursing officer), "Well, I think it helped us to say, wait a minute, this really is chaotic." Correia herself observed,

> And what we figured sitting through that event, listening to the nurses, and going up on the floor and watching nurses try to get a patient from the beginning to the end—that it was really heroics. Coming in, the plans were very vague about what was going to happen to that patient. Everyone had their own plan.

A physician added that the process was revealing for everyone: "It was a big *aha* that helped make visible to us that we were not doing patient care as well as we would like."

Through discovery, members gained clarity. Their beliefs about delivering care in an integrated and patient-focused manner did not square with actual practice. Nor did those beliefs seem suited to undergirding how they would have to deliver care in the future if they were to provide the quality of care they aspired to. Their ability to *make new sense* of the mapping difficulties supported members' continuing move toward embracing new beliefs.

In the wake of their experience, the group coalesced around the new belief that they needed to minimize the obstacles that caused fragmentation in care ("new belief" in Figure 2.2), including the traditional clinical roles and siloed units in the current delivery model. A new belief in minimizing obstacles as a means to better serving patients reshaped members' ideas about care delivery and how to improve it.

The new belief energized members. They resolved to proceed by examining potential obstacles. Moreover, because in-patient care was "so broken," they would begin immediately with that area, moving subsequently to other care areas. Susan Walker (project manager) commented: "We quickly realized that we couldn't work on all disconnects in care at once." Rodgers concurred: "When we looked at inpatient care issues, our first big *aha* was, if we don't fix inpatient care, we can't do the rest of it."

This was not, however, the end of their discovery process. It would take multiple cycles of discovery for them to discover what they still didn't know about care delivery and use it to create their new innovative care model that would produce outstanding patient and staff outcomes. In the end, their work would win national acclaim.

What's particularly significant in the DeltaCare case is that Correia and the group members didn't get defeated by frustration or irritation. That could have trapped them in old beliefs. They could have derailed the process. Instead, they boldly pursued discovery, through thick and thin, to a productive endpoint. That assured they made the jump from an *inability to make sense* of their situation to an *ability to make new sense* of the once nebulous situation. The mapping difficulties turned obstacles into opportunity. They overcame their old habits of expectation to discover a novel way forward to transform their delivery of patient care.

THE STORY OF DISCOVERY

The case of DeltaCare reads like a classic organizational success story, and that's for good reason. It opens with a stakeholder group that—over time, against several complications, facing tough odds—overcomes issues to emerge with success. If you're a leader facing this kind of daunting challenge, you might even think of yourself as a protagonist going through a similar sequence of events. Driven by the process of discovery throughout, you and everyone involved work together to create fundamentally new ways of operating.

Your effectiveness as that protagonist—as catalyst, guide, and co-author of discovery—depends on how well you write the story with others so that your collective process generates insights. Together, you learn and grow as you deepen your understanding of the unsettled situation. You struggle for new meaning about the unsettling situation and embrace new beliefs that better suit the new reality.

You learn in the process that you can't consider ignoring a belief-shaking new reality. You can't think about explaining it away or censoring it. If you're writing your own story of discovery, you rise to and confront beliefs that have lost their basis in dealing with new realities. Despite feelings of discomfort with the unknown, you question what you hold dear and forge ahead, seeking and gaining insights, and generating new ways to deal with the realities.

In the end, your story will not feel so uncomfortable. That's because the story of cultivating discovery with others to create something new is basic to human striving in all realms. In the end, all stories of successful discovery bring clarity to the once ill-fitting pieces of your understanding about the unsettled situations. They reveal new trajectories to once unimagined places, guided by the reoriented beliefs and practices. They spur actionable and desired paths forward that you can have confidence in. You are full of hope for the new, desired future.

If you don't see yourself pursuing this storyline—if you try to jump to a conclusion, if you try to discover the new formula without undertaking the discovery process—you will fail to triumph over your challenges. You will not break from rigidity of belief in the face of new realities. You will not unlock the human capacity for seeing the world anew and for embracing new beliefs and practices that make that world better.

Helping you write the story of discovery as a process experienced with others is what the rest of this book is about. The process of discovery will become your ultimate resource in working with colleagues to create change, or a sequence of changes that bring something fundamentally new into being—just like what Microsoft and DeltaCare have relied on to create a new culture and new model of care delivery. Like Correia and Nadella, you will spur discovery processes that generate positive impact not only in the organization but beyond. In the next chapters, you'll find out how—how you will write full and gratifying discovery stories of your own and with others.

~~~~~

1. As an individual, how do you typically respond when confronted with new realities that challenge your beliefs? Do you hold fast to your current beliefs, embrace new beliefs, or stand somewhere in-between?
2. Identify a new reality that challenged taken-for-granted beliefs in your organization. These could be beliefs about leading people. About market success. About where to work. Or others. How did the organization respond to the challenge? Was discovery encouraged? What actions supported this? What actions derailed it?
3. In your opinion, what does it take to move toward new beliefs and new ways of operating?

NOTES

1 Bryant, Adam. 2014 (February 20). "Satya Nadella, Chief of Microsoft, on His New Role." *New York Times Corner Office*. Interview. www.nytimes.com/2014/02/21/business/satya-nadella-chief-of-microsoft-on-his-new-role.html, accessed June 2023.

2. This figure reached 221,000 in 2022.
3. Bryant, Adam. 2014 (February 20). "Satya Nadella, Chief of Microsoft, on His New Role." *New York Times Corner Office*. Interview. www.nytimes.com/2014/02/21/business/satya-nadella-chief-of-microsoft-on-his-new-role.html, accessed June 2023.
4. Developed by the psychologist Carol Dweck, growth mindset is a belief that human abilities such as talent are malleable and can improve with effort, practice, and input from others. Refer to Dweck's classic book first published in 2006: *Mindset: The New Psychology of Success*. New York: Ballantine Books.
5. Ibarra, Herminia, Aneeta Rattan, & Anna Johnston. 2018. "Satya Nadella at Microsoft: Instilling a Growth Mindset." London Business School Case CS-18-008:7.
6. Ibid., 5.
7. Shibu, Sherin, & Shana Lebowitz. 2019. "Microsoft Is Rolling Out a New Management Framework to Its Leaders." *Business Insider*. www.businessinsider.com/microsoftis-using-growth-mindset-to-power-management-strategy-2019-11?r=US&IR=T, accessed June 2023.
8. Mautz, Scott. 2019 (November 21). "Microsoft Leaders Are Asked to Showcase Three Skills." *Inc Magazine*. Blog. www.inc.com/scott-mautz/microsoft-leaders-areasked-to-showcase-3-skills-recent-psychology-research-says-you-should-too.html, accessed June 2023.
9. Mayer, Kathryn. 2021 (October 6). "How the HR Executive of the Year Rebooted Microsoft's Culture." *Human Resource Executive*. https://hrexecutive.com/how-thehr-executive-of-the-year-rebooted-microsofts-culture/, accessed June 2023.
10. Ibid.
11. Economist. 2020 (October 24). "How Satya Nadella Turned Microsoft Around: Now for the Hard Part."
12. Wall Street Journal. www.wsj.com/market-data/quotes/MSFT.
13. Murray, Matt. 2019 (August 6). "Future of Work: Davos." *Wall Street Journal*. Interview. www.wsj.com/video/events/future-of-work-davos/BE0D0E6C-87E1-4A3F-B4A4-8F6FA4BEA1B4.html, accessed June 2023.
14. Peirce, Charles Sanders. 1931–1958. *The Collected Papers of Charles Sanders Peirce*, Vols. 1–8. Edited by C. Hartshorne, P. Weiss, & A.W. Burks. Cambridge: Harvard University Press.
15. The definition of habit as disposition to act is grounded in pragmatism thought, particularly Charles Peirce. By recognizing that it is single ways, not acts that constitute habit, Peirce led the way for habits to be conceived as conditional in nature. Thus, alterable through creative action.
16. Peirce, Charles Sanders. 1877. "The Fixation of Belief." *Popular Science Monthly* 12:1–15. Fixation of belief highlights stability and immovability associated with rigidly adhering to beliefs.
17. Peirce, Charles Sanders. 1931–1958. *The Essential Peirce: Selected Philosophical Writings*. Edited by C. Hartshorne, P. Weiss, & A.W. Burks. Peirce Edition Project. Bloomington: Indiana University Press.
18. DeltaCare is a horizontally integrated, nonprofit health system located in the United States. At the time of the research, it consisted of multiple hospitals and approximately 6,000 staff and clinicians. With the exception of hospital system president, Kathryn Correia, the names of the organization and staff used in this chapter are pseudonyms.

19 The data for the DeltaCare story includes interviews, archival documents, external media, and observation, discussed in my publication: Golden-Biddle, Karen A. 2020. "Discovery as Abductive Mechanism for Reorienting Habits within Organizational Change." *Academy of Management Journal* 63(6):1951–1975. They are being used with the permission of the Academy of Management.
20 DeltaCare used lean methodology. In this methodology, the event is named, an enterprise-wide, value stream. For the purposes of discovery, the selection of a similar methodology needs to be experience-based, involving practical activity. It should not be abstract discussion.
21 DeltaCare managers and clinicians received full pay during this event.
22 Pragmatists suggest this early exploration is an important attempt to discover the "diffusely problematic quality" (Joas, Hans. 1996. *The Creativity of Action*. Chicago: University of Chicago Press, p. 131) of situations that have become unsettled.

REFERENCES

Bryant, Adam. 2014 (February 20). "Satya Nadella, Chief of Microsoft, On His New Role." *New York Times Corner Office*. Interview. www.nytimes.com/2014/02/21/business/satya-nadella-chief-of-microsoft-on-his-new-role.html, accessed June 2023.

Dweck, Carol. 2006. *Mindset: The New Psychology of Success*. New York: Ballantine Books.

Economist. 2020 (October 24). "How Satya Nadella Turned Microsoft Around: Now for the Hard Part."

Golden-Biddle, Karen A. 2020. "Discovery as Abductive Mechanism for Reorienting Habits within Organizational Change." *Academy of Management Journal* 63(6): 1951–1975.

Ibarra, Herminia, Aneeta Rattan, & Anna Johnston. 2018. "Satya Nadella at Microsoft: Instilling a Growth Mindset." London Business School Case CS-18-008:7.

Joas, Hans. 1996. *The Creativity of Action*. Chicago: University of Chicago Press.

Mautz, Scott. 2019 (November 21). "Microsoft Leaders Are Asked to Showcase Three Skills." *Inc Magazine*. Blog. www.inc.com/scott-mautz/microsoft-leaders-are-asked-to-showcase-3-skills-recent-psychology-research-says-you-should-too.html, accessed June 2023.

Mayer, Kathryn. 2021 (October 6). "How the HR Executive of the Year Rebooted Microsoft's Culture." *Human Resource Executive*. https://hrexecutive.com/how-thehr-executive-of-the-year-rebooted-microsofts-culture/, accessed June 2023.

Murray, Matt. 2019 (August 6). "Future of Work: Davos." *Wall Street Journal*. Interview. www.wsj.com/video/events/future-of-work-davos/BE0D0E6C-87E1-4A3F-B4A48F6FA4BEA1B4.html, accessed June 2023.

Peirce, Charles Sanders. 1877. "The Fixation of Belief." *Popular Science Monthly* 12:1–15.

Peirce, Charles Sanders. 1931–1958a. *The Collected Papers of Charles Sanders Peirce*, Vols. 1–8. Edited by C. Hartshorne, P. Weiss, & A.W. Burks. Cambridge: Harvard University Press.

Peirce, Charles Sanders. 1931–1958b. *The Essential Peirce: Selected Philosophical Writings*. Edited by C. Hartshorne, P. Weiss, & A.W. Burks. Peirce Edition Project. Bloomington: Indiana University Press.

Shibu, Sherin, & Shana Lebowitz. 2019. "Microsoft Is Rolling Out a New Management Framework to Its Leaders." *Business Insider*. www.businessinsider.com/microsoftis-using-growth-mindset-to-power-management-strategy-2019–11?r=US&IR=T, accessed June 2023.

Capitalizing on Surprise

Doug Dietz, an industrial designer and principal design thinker at General Electric Healthcare Innovation Lab, had just finished two years of leading a team of designers to develop a new MRI scanner. Dietz recalls being "very proud" of the award-winning machine that had incorporated factors to make the machine better for the technologist.

But that pride was not to last long. Early in the launch of their new MRI scanner design, Dietz received an invitation to visit a hospital to see it in operation. What he experienced stung him to the core. He had expected the machine to be well received. But how the device worked in the hospital deeply surprised him. What's more, it transformed his belief about how to do design work altogether.

During his visit, a technologist asked Dietz to step into the hallway for a short while because a patient was coming in. He made way for a family with a child. "I could tell as the family got closer that the little girl was . . . weeping," Dietz recalls. The father was leaning down and saying to his daughter, "Remember. We've talked about this. You can be brave."[1]

He followed the family into the MRI room. Standing behind the girl, Dietz could see she was frozen. "Looking into this same environment that I was just standing in," he recalls, "I realized that this is [now] something totally different." The walls were painted a dull beige. A danger sticker was posted by the machine. To the girl, the MRI scanner "looked like a brick with a hole in it"—not the "elegant, sleek piece of technology" he had taken so much pride in.[2]

DOI: 10.4324/9781003513681-4

The technician darkened the room. The girl started to break down. The terror in the girl and anxiety in the parents was palpable. The machine's size and clattering—in a dark room—terrified her. Worse, the technician called the anesthesiologist to sedate the girl, a practice he learned was routine for more than 80 percent of young patients.[3]

Dietz recalls the session as "a huge awakening." To be sure, he and his design team had sized the machine for children. That was a plus, but now a minor one. They had overlooked the experience of patients, their families, and hospital staff. The experience "shocked" him.

In the course of just this one visit, Dietz had experienced two gut-wrenching surprises: a tearful girl aside distressed parents and an anesthesiologist administering a sedative so a patient could withstand the stress imposed by his invention. He recalls being "choked up." How could he have expected accolades for creating this award-winning machine?

Dietz was at a loss to interpret the surprises in light of his prevailing beliefs. In a sense, as he later admitted to his wife, he was as distressed professionally as he had ever been.

So, what would you expect Dietz to do once back among his award-winning team? What would his teammates think? What would a team of technologists think at most companies? Ignore the surprise! That's what often happens. It's the overwhelming temptation people experience, and not just executives but as people at every level in organizations. The early accolades for the technology outweigh the gravity of later experience.

My research shows that, with work to do and deadlines to meet, people push aside such unexpected new realities all the time. They do so because they are able to fall back on one, two, or even all three of the discovery derailers: they ignore the surprise and go back to more pressing work; they explain away other possibilities to respond to the surprise; or they remain stuck with their initial beliefs as best, refuting all others. They don't take even the first step necessary to ignite the discovery process: valuing surprise.

We can credit Dietz for not hesitating to take that step. He could have spurned the idea. After all, he had designed a machine that operated perfectly. He had hit his design goals, and hospitals eagerly sought the design. He could also have dismissed the experience of just one child. He had plenty of room to sustain his current beliefs—and overlook the opportunity to discover a new productive course forward.

But he would not have felt good about the product. How could he feel fine when he could see how it negatively affected children? That discomfort is common when people experience surprise. That's because nobody can feel completely comfortable when surprising experience calls into question their prevailing beliefs. They sense at least intuitively that not only their plans and behaviors might be wrong, but also their beliefs. Yet, the derailers allow them to skirt the discomfort, staying the course of the status quo. They don't address the surprise. They stay stuck in rigidity of belief.

The failure to take stock of and value surprise leads to untold lost opportunities for people, customers, and organizations. While it's true that surprising events and experiences do encourage people to move away from prior beliefs and leverage the motor of surprise, "work gets in the way," and people put out the spark. The surprise then doesn't help transform the unsettled situation into a desired, new one.

Dietz didn't take this path. Instead, he realized that the earlier situation had suddenly become unsettled and difficult to decipher. The success factors he had focused on before didn't add up in light of new realities. What used to work like clockwork no longer did. In recognizing this, he embraced surprise, which allowed him to loosen the hold on his prior design beliefs. That was when he ignited the discovery process. His experience shows how anyone can reject the derailers and put themselves on the road to substantive change.

SURPRISE: DISCOVERY'S FIRST MOTOR

Most leaders are taught to run their organizations with reliable, predictable results. They don't like "surprise." If you're one of them, you're not likely to think of surprise as a friend. Surprise upends situations you consider settled. You have worked hard to be sure you and your team know how to think and act. When surprise disrupts that confidence, you see it as an unwanted and threatening interloper. It can put you in an awkward, even destabilizing, position of uncertainty, facing events or results you didn't expect.

As a leader, you're not inclined to admit that you've been surprised. You're not supposed to be taken off guard. You're not supposed to feel at a loss for direction. You're being asked to explore something that seems illogical or unworkable. That leads to a feeling in your gut,

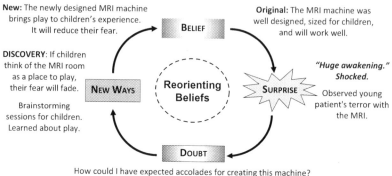

FIGURE 3.1 Redesigning the MRI machine.

sometimes subtle and niggly, sometimes intense like that experienced by Dietz. The feeling affects you physically. You expected the current situation to turn out as usual, or at least different in a way you could control. You don't want to face the fact that the surprise signals that your beliefs could be in error. Yet, you feel the confrontation between your beliefs (habits of expectation) and your experience.

But this unsettling clash is exactly what makes surprise such a powerful engine in kicking off discovery. Figure 3.1 sketches out the cycle of discovery you're about to undertake. This is a journey everyone has to take to succeed at discovery and make their organization and world better. It is a personal and an organizational journey. It begins with one set of beliefs that no longer work in light of new realities or other challenging situations. It proceeds with an evolution in your thinking to a reoriented set of beliefs. Without your leadership team and employees, migrating from ill-fitting beliefs today to well-fitting ones tomorrow, you cannot change needed practices or processes. You cannot alter obsolete work designs. You cannot transform organizational cultures.

My research confirms that belief change evolves through the cycle of discovery and its three phases: capitalizing on surprise, harnessing genuine doubt, and launching new ways. These are not distinct, strictly sequential phases. Rather, you iterate through them as you discover and firm up beliefs that fit for ongoing success. Nor do the three phases take place on their own. As a leader, you need to facilitate them. You need to treat them as three motors you can engage with others to power the change. There are no shortcuts. Without going through the full cycle, people's beliefs don't change. Discovery is derailed. With discovery as partner, you can imagine a whole organization that relishes surprise.

In this chapter, we begin with the motor of surprise, how to use it to grapple with unexpected realities that operate *contrary to your prevailing beliefs*.[4] This is a time when the lack of fit, appropriately addressed, explodes into your awareness. Ironically, an unsettling situation that signals you need to attend to surprising developments becomes the doorway to your future—just as the surprising developments in that darkened room led to a new future for Dietz.

Surprise Compels a Special Reasoning

The mere act of entertaining surprise has more power than you might think. Confronted by surprise, you eschew certainty of conviction. That frees you to seek more tentative and flexible means to generate potential explanations to the surprising experience. You're able to tap the forces of abduction—a special kind of reasoning[5] that drives insight, *ahas*, hypotheses, conjectures, new ideas.

In contrast to the long-standing logic of deduction, which "proves that something *must be*, and induction, which shows something *actually* is operative, the logic of abduction merely suggests that something *may be*."[6] By using it, you engage in inventive processes. For example, you know to seek clues to the surprising experience. Clues that inform your guesses, speculations, and conjectures about the new reality and what it might mean in your environment. The inventive reasoning equips you to productively engage surprise and capitalize on the insights yielded.

You can see how this worked with Dietz. He tapped abductive reasoning in his search to understand the clash between the disturbing surprises and his beliefs about quality design. His search started with the realization that he had let down "the very patients he was trying to help."[7] Dietz could have let belief rigidity take hold by trying to defend his machine. Instead, he furthered his flexibility of belief by embracing surprise. Why, he wondered, didn't he discover more about the conditions of the machine in use *before* he and his team designed it?

Surprise Gives Rise to a New Story

Surprise has power because embracing it forces you to search for a plausible story that could drive transformation of the puzzling situation. How might you reorient this unsettled, ill-defined, and unworkable situation into a new, intelligible, and actionable one? How might that situation become a springboard to your future? The time has come to write a new story of what the desired future and your new ways of operating look like.

Surprise, then, is the catalyst to help you move away from prior beliefs and toward new ones. It accelerates and generates discoveries in many forms—insights, alternative perspectives, new hypotheses, novel ideas. As it drives new understanding, it can change how you feel, reshape your goals and desires, and affect your hopes for the future. It can be aspirational. From it comes hints of new, workable beliefs, which can contribute to your changing culture, behaviors, and practices.

In the weeks following his hospital visit, Dietz sought input from trusted colleagues and friends both inside and outside General Electric. He didn't have the funding to redesign the device, but he could focus on reimagining the setting and experience. That led him to seek ways to see the situation through children's eyes. For example, he ran brainstorming sessions at a daycare, involving children, the director, a team from a children's museum, and other GE customers. The children loved taking "three kitchen chairs and a blanket to build a fort, castle, boat, shelter, truck you name it," he recalls.[8] They would play with it forever.

This and other observations spurred abductive thinking—and ignited an *aha*: if he could get children to think of the MRI room as a place to play and imagine—something natural for them—their fear would probably fade. That discovery was the genesis and fuel of GE's new "Adventure" MRI series. "Adventures" using fun characters, aromatherapy, and visuals would bring play to the children's experience. The result was dramatic: a reduction in children needing sedation, lower anxiety for kids and parents while increasing productivity, and increased patient satisfaction.

Dietz's story is a universal story. You may have lived a story of this kind yourself, experiencing a time when your world of work no longer operated in a way that functioned well, owing to the advent of new realities. If you focused on discovery, you didn't let the derailers stop you. You engaged with surprise. You challenged prior beliefs. You replaced them with new ones that quieted that churning stomach and fed a sense of opportunity in taking the surprise to heart.

The universal story is also one of how, by developing flexibility of belief and embracing surprise, people anywhere in any organization can ignite a discovery process. That was not just true for Dietz, whose flexibility of belief allowed him to see that the world of design didn't factor in empathy for end users. It was true for the people at DeltaCare, the clinicians and leaders, whose flexibility revealed that the world of healthcare didn't value a patient-centric, integrated delivery structure. And it was true for Microsoft leadership and employees, whose flexibility revealed how their organizational culture didn't support the beliefs and practices that enabled innovation.

For each of these organizations, the new story brought coherence and future orientation to the once ill-fitting understanding about the new realities and unsettled situations. It fueled new beliefs. It revealed new trajectories. It helped them craft new actionable paths forward that everyone has confidence in.

Surprise Insists on Flexibility

One challenge that leaders face in writing a successful story is that, too easily, everyone slips back into prevailing beliefs. You have probably experienced this yourself. You face a pivotal decision: Do you ignite that spark of discovery or put it out? You choose to snuff the catalytic spark, because you have in mind another way of dealing with the unsettled situation. When that happens, however, your fixed approach becomes a barrier to you and your organization breaking out on a new trajectory.

Fundamentally different ways of working don't emerge magically, out of the blue. When you're the leader, you need to take extra measures to activate the three motors. The key practice? Develop that flexibility of belief as a managerial and behavioral mindset. At the core of that mindset, obviously enough, you have to be willing to shun the discovery derailers, making a point to model the nonuse of derailers and support others' efforts to do the same.

This modeling means you don't ignore unsettling clues. Nor do you explain away discrepancies. And you don't censor contrary ideas. By *not* taking action that would otherwise derail discovery, you also start to develop flexibility of belief, an essential part of cultivating discovery. Although straightforward in theory, this principle is nevertheless difficult to put into consistent use. It requires everyone to acknowledge, rather than reactively dismiss, unexpected new realities.

DISCOVERY ENABLERS: CAPITALIZING ON SURPRISE

It's no wonder that many leaders mishandle surprise and double down on or return to prevailing beliefs and ways of operating. Although surprises pop up every day in our work and personal lives—and despite the centrality of handling them well during transformation—they pose a tough challenge for anyone who hasn't cultivated flexible responses to surprise that ignite discovery.

If you're one of those people, that's understandable. Your mishandling stems in part from not adequately preparing to handle surprise in a flexible way. When surprise triggers uncertainty, you instead take one of two responses: avoid or adapt. Either way, you regard surprise as negative, a harbinger of uncertainty and a failure of intelligence.[9] And your first impulse is not to be flexible at all.[10] If not, you try to neutralize or get rid of it. You also seek to prevent surprises from happening in the first place. From that stems the drive to develop "more reliable and predictable organizations."[11]

The philosophy of "no-surprise management" encourages everyone to prevent surprise by controlling circumstances. Research shows that even in the process of innovation, some teams prefer to avoid surprise. Researchers Robert Austin, Lee Devin, and Erin Sullivan[12] conducted a study of whether and how innovators integrated unexpected events into their work. One of the cases—a product team in a manufacturing group—illustrated what researchers called "a general tendency to avoid surprises." A short interview exchange between a researcher and team member captures this tendency:

Question: Objective is to avoid surprises?
Answer: Yeah, I wish I could someday come up with a project that had no surprises.
Question: So, surprises are always bad?
Answer: Most of the time.[13]

In the second response to surprise, adapting to it, you're still often likely to mishandle it. That's because you regard surprise as blocking ongoing work. You do recognize it as an inherent feature of complex organizations, but that can ironically lead to another counterproductive response. Since surprises "cannot be avoided, eliminated or controlled,"[14] you adapt by fixing what led to it, for example, implementing strategies to boost revenue in the midst of decline. You then move on as quickly as possible.

The urge to move on causes its own harms. Consider the study[15] of pilot experiences of surprise in the cockpit by Amy Rankin, Rogier Woltjer, and Joris Field. Their research shows that flight crews miss valuable information all the time. Instead of engaging in discovery, they gather evidence that supports an initial hypothesis and confirms the first viable solution.

That's not to say that strategies to avoid or cope with surprise never serve as necessary functions in organizations. But used consistently, such responses also reinforce prevailing beliefs and rigidity. Most leaders would do better to focus less on strategies to deal with surprise as an annoyance and focus more on strategies to deal with it as an opportunity. Surprise deserves to be cherished as that first motor of success. To capitalize on surprise for discovery, leaders need to model and support a discovery-oriented response. This requires that leaders and other inquirers know how to use discovery enablers that relax belief rigidity and encourage the release of ill-fitting beliefs.

Three discovery enablers will help you engage with surprise to win all the benefits of discovery. Without these enablers, you and your organization may remain inclined toward efficiency, prediction, and staying the course. Only with them do you relax rigidity of belief and encourage the release of ill-fitting beliefs. Only with them do you break through suppression and intentionally cultivate discovery.

Savoring Surprise

The first enabler is savoring surprise. Although surprise is all around us, and although experience teaches us new things by means of surprise, we don't necessarily recognize surprises for what they are. Sometimes they take a while to reveal their rich insights and opportunities. A good example comes from the experience of Scott Cook and his team at Intuit, a business software company.

In 1984, shortly after Intuit launched its home financial product Quicken, CEO Cook and his team surveyed customers to learn about who was using their software. One of the questions they asked was where customers were when they used Quicken. About half replied that they used it in an office. Cook's response? "That's weird. We built a home product. They're probably just taking their bills into the office because they don't have a computer."[16] The team didn't think more about it.

That is, until follow-up surveys showed again the same statistic: about half of the respondents used Quicken software in the office. Even then Cook thought: "It made no sense. We ignored it. I ignored it."[17] After a few more years, the stillunexpected, yet now-persistent survey response started to nag at Cook. Why, he asked, are people "answering this question wrong?"

Up to this point, Cook and his team had responded to the surprising experience like many people do. They make the oddity familiar—like they did with their reasoning that customers using the software in the office must not have a computer at home. Their rigidity kept them fixed on the belief that customers of Quicken should be using the product at home, not at the office. They derailed discovery by explaining away the discrepant result and missing the full potential of the surprise.

But the surprising results continued to cause Cook unease. The team finally broke through their rigidity of belief by pressing on to look for new explanations to the surprising results. They even went to their customers' workplaces to observe what they were doing. There they learned something that didn't make sense to them—something they "had never imagined." Customers were using Quicken, a home product, to keep the books for their small businesses.

That's when they discovered the "key problem" that had remained invisible to them. Their prevailing belief—that the only way to keep written records of business finances was by using formal accounting methods—clashed with the ways customers actually practiced accounting in small businesses. Said Cook, "something else was true, different from our own beliefs." That insight led in turn to the development and launch of QuickBooks, which remains the company's major product.

"Only when we started focusing on it [the surprise], savoring the surprise, did we discover this giant market opportunity,"[18] said Cook in an *Inc.* magazine article decades later.

As Cook's experience suggests, in today's competitive markets, ignoring surprise for months or years puts the whole organization at risk. The time has come to savor the occurrence of surprises, instead of ignoring them. Savor them, instead of explaining them away. Savoring surprise builds the flexibility of belief essential for letting go of old beliefs and taking on new ones, and for creating something new that was previously unimaginable.

Seeking Clues to Surprise

The second enabler is seeking clues that inform conjecture and guessing about what that unexpected experience could mean in your environment. Such clues can be explicit anomalies, like Dietz's image of the terrified young girl and her parents approaching the MRI room. Or they can be mere hints of something unexpected such as the difficulties in mapping care flows experienced by DeltaCare members. Teams can use the various clues to make tentative assessments about the surprising experience.

Imagine teams of scientists at work on the complex endeavor of discovering new drugs. Organizational researchers Danielle Dunne and Deborah Dougherty conducted a study of such innovators[19] in biopharmaceutical companies. The findings showed that many scientists used clues to develop a tentative, and possibly even incorrect, configuration of interactions between the potential drug and the process by which it worked in the human body against the focal disease. The provisional nature of the configuration supported their use of the special, abductive logic for discovery. For example, they would "delve into details" while remaining "open to unexpected insights."[20] And they would engage in "going down a path you don't know what it will be."[21]

This example shows how critical seeking clues is to capitalizing on surprise because it can lead to what is not known as well as inform possible ways to a new known. To implement this discovery enabler, you start by seeking clues to the surprising experience. Then, like the scientists, you use those clues flexibly and hypothetically to discover a world in which that clue becomes meaningful and gives meaning.[22]

Dietz did just that when he sought clues to the surprising experience and used them in wrestling with his feelings and questions. How could he have missed the child's experience in designing the MRI? By Dietz's own admission, he had been so focused on the "shiny object" he had designed that he "totally missed the whole picture."[23] He then used clues, now gathered with the perspective and situation of the young girl and her family in mind—the dull beige walls, the metaphor of the machine like a brick with a hole in it, the extremely high sedation rates—to conjecture a new world in which the image of the young girl and her family became meaningful in his environment. And that led to the discovery of the new "Adventure Series" design for the MRI machine. Later, while in a conversation with the mother of a six-year-old daughter who had undergone a scan in the newly designed machine (a pirate ship), the daughter came over to them and said, "Mommy, can we come back tomorrow?"[24]

When you seek clues to surprise, you create a world in which the surprise becomes meaningful. This is not a one-step process, from surprise to explanation. In keeping with the iterative nature of discovery, such clues and background information point to tentative proposals for transforming the unsettled situation into a new one. In the face of surprise, you guess, conjecture, hypothesize, speculate, assess plausibility, with clues using the special discovery logic—to build a new future from one upended with new realities. Along the way, you build flexibility of belief so that the next time, you find yourself in an even better position to seek clues to surprise.

Setting Surprise in Motion

In addition to capitalizing on naturally occurring situations of surprise, a third enabler is setting in motion the opportunity for surprise to occur. Leaders do this by organizing experience that could generate an unexpected confrontation between prior beliefs and new realities.

That's what Kathryn Correia, along with clinicians and other leaders in DeltaCare, did. Rather than just discussing patient care flows, the group members mapped them on flipcharts. When disconnects surfaced, they were taken aback. Not sure if the disconnects in the exercise were real, the group members decided to take a close-up look by walking actual care flows with patients as much as possible. To their deep chagrin, they observed how patients, especially the most vulnerable ones, struggled with their delivery system. Their experience clashed with their beliefs that they were delivering integrated care. And this all happened because they took on a process to surface a range of surprises that they had been totally unaware of, which in turn led them to transform their delivery system.

In 2013 Aron Ain, CEO of Kronos, an innovative workforce management company founded in 1977 and now part of ÜKG, set in motion his own process for surfacing surprise. He challenged his newly established off-site team: "If you were going to start a company that was going to compete with Kronos, what would you do? How would it work?" The goal of this challenge? To design a "brand new and completely different product" that would shake up the industry. Ain told the team, "We have a year to go try and figure this out." The group looked at him and said, "Impossible!"[25]

The surprising creation and tight timeline of the team challenged everyone's beliefs about being a traditional license-based company.[26] They needed to discover a novel way to put Kronos out of business before another company could. Through their work, the group produced the novel concept for Workforce Dimensions, the first cloud and mobile-based, AI-powered workforce management suite. In disrupting themselves, they discovered the new way forward—away from license-based beliefs about business and toward new beliefs associated with operating as a cloud business.[27]

Satya Nadella set surprise in motion, too, when, for the first time in company history, he invited the senior leadership of recently acquired companies to a retreat for the top 150 corporate executives. "These new Microsoft leaders," said Nadella, "were mission-oriented, innovative, born in the mobile-first and cloud-first world. I knew we could learn from their fresh, outside perspective." Through the participation of these recent outsiders—an unexpected new reality for the executives—the retreat illuminated the clash between the prior beliefs of Microsoft and anticipated, new ones. Nadella encouraged the founders to share their experience of operating in the new mobile and cloud worlds. Nadella described the interaction with the founders: "They asked questions. They shared their own journeys. They pushed us to be better."[28]

More than savoring surprise or spotting clues to it, setting surprise in motion is the most proactive and purposeful discovery enabler. It requires leaders and team members to cultivate the flexibility of belief that prepares and equips them to have their beliefs upended. That is when organization members position themselves to be surprised and gain insight through the discovery process.

SUMMARY

Discovery is at the heart of human effort to create something new and better out of a new reality or unexpected situation that upends prevailing beliefs. The human quality needed to achieve this is flexibility of belief, as the stories show. You cultivate this quality by using discovery enablers throughout the cycle, beginning with the first motor of surprise.

Although surprise is critical and necessary, it is not enough by itself to yield the benefits of discovery. Not sufficient to generate the insights, imagined worlds, and other inventive resources that people create. You need to build on the motor of surprise with the next two motors in writing the arc of your story of discovery. Your feelings of surprise provide a fertile ground for progress. They prompt you to harness genuine doubt, the subject of the next chapter, and then launch new ways, the subject of chapter 5. When you actively deploy the three motors together, you let go of ill-fitting beliefs that no longer work with new realities. And you search for new beliefs and practices that do. That's when you and your team grasp holistically how to cultivate discovery on a more consistent basis. Together, you embrace discovery and its many cycles in creating new ways of operating.

~~~~~

1. How do you respond when you experience something surprising that challenges your beliefs? Do you resist it? Ignore it? Maybe savor it?
2. What discovery enablers (i.e., savor surprise, seek clues to surprise, and set surprise in motion) have you seen people in your organization use in response to an unexpected experience? What happened?
3. Select one discovery enabler from this chapter. Imagine using that enabler more consistently. What actions do you take? How do you feel when using it? What thoughts run through your mind?

NOTES

1 Kelly, David, & Tom Kelly. 2013. "The Journey from Design Thinking to Creative Confidence. *IDEO*. Blog. www.ideou.com/blogs/inspiration/from-design-thinking to-creative-confidence, accessed June 2023. Adapted from chapter 1 in the book *Creative Confidence*. New York: Crown Business Publishers. The award (2009) for Dietz's MRI machine from the Industrial Designers Society of America is located here: www.idsa.org/awards/idea/medical-scientific-products/discovery-mr
2 Dietz, Doug. 2012. "Transforming Healthcare for Children and Their Families." *TEDxSanJoseCA*. Video. www.youtube.com/watch?v=-jajduxPD6H4, accessed June 2023; Ogle, Jason. 2018 (January 31). "The Life-Changing Impact of Empathy in Design." *Medium*. Blog. https://medium.com/user-defenders/theimpact-of-empathy-in-design-b55c3157d070, accessed June 2023.
3 Bolton, Guy. 2016 (January 21). "By Turning Medical Scans into Adventures, GE Eases Children's Fears." *Milwaukee Journal Sentinel*. https://archive.jsonline. com/business/by-turning-medical-scansinto-adventures-ge-eases-childrens-fearsb99647870z1–366161191.html, accessed June 2023.

4 To spur change, surprise must disturb how people think things are supposed to happen, as it did with Dietz. You realize that something is incongruous, requiring you to puzzle through to figure out what it means.
5 The "special" logic refers to abductive logic, a conjectural mode of inquiry first articulated by the pragmatist philosopher, Charles Peirce. People use abductive logic to make sense of surprising observations or facts. This form of logic shapes the process of discovery developed in this book. See: Golden-Biddle, Karen A. 2020. "Discovery as Abductive Mechanism for Reorienting Habits within Organizational Change." *Academy of Management Journal* 63(6):1951–1975.
6 Locke, Karen, Karen Golden-Biddle, & Martha S. Feldman. 2008. "Making Doubt Generative: Rethinking the Role of Doubt in the Research Process." *Organization Science* 19(6):907.
7 Kelly, David, & Tom Kelly. 2013. "The Journey from Design Thinking to Creative Confidence. *IDEO*. Blog. www.ideou.com/blogs/inspiration/from-design-thinking-to-creative-confidence, accessed June 2023.
8 Dietz, Doug. 2012. "Transforming Healthcare for Children and Their Families." *TEDxSanJoseCA*. Video. www.youtube.com/watch?v=jajduxPD6H4, accessed June 2023.
9 Lampel, Joseph, & Zur Shapira. 2001. "Judgmental Errors, Interactive Norms, and the Difficulty of Detecting Strategic Surprises." *Organization Science* 12(5):599–611.
10 Cunha, Miguel Pinae, Stewart R. Clegg, & Ken Kamoche. 2006. "Surprises in Management and Organization: Concept, Sources, and a Typology." *British Journal of Management* 17:317–329. See also: McDaniel, Reuben R., Michelle E. Jordan, & Brigitte F. Fleeman. 2003. "Surprise, Surprise, Surprise! A Complexity Science View of the Unexpected." *Health Care Management Review* 28:266–278.
11 McDaniel, Reuben R., Michelle E. Jordan, & Brigitte F. Fleeman. 2003. "Surprise, Surprise, Surprise! A Complexity Science View of the Unexpected." *Health Care Management Review* 28:266.
12 Austin, Robert Daniel, Lee Devin, & E.E. Sullivan. 2012. "Accidental Innovation: Supporting Valuable Unpredictability in the Creative Process." *Organization Science* 23(5):1505–1522.
13 Ibid., 1510.
14 McDaniel, Reuben R., Michelle E. Jordan, & Brigitte F. Fleeman. 2003. "Surprise, Surprise, Surprise! A Complexity Science View of the Unexpected." *Health Care Management Review* 28:266.
15 Rankin, Amy, Rogier Woltjer, & Joris Field. 2016. "Sensemaking Following Surprise in the Cockpit – A Re-Framing Problem." *Cognition, Technology and Work* 18:623–642.
16 Cook, Scott. 2015 (November 4). "Savor the Surprises" (Presentation in a course). *Stanford eCorner*. Video. http://ecorner.stanford.edu/videos/3597/Savor-the-Surprises, accessed June 2023.
17 Ibid.
18 Winfrey, Graham. 2014 (July 25). "Intuit's Scott Cook on the Surprising Sources of Massive Growth." *Inc Magazine*. www.inc.com/graham-winfrey/intuit-s-scott-cook-on-savoring-surprises.html, accessed June 2023.
19 Dunne, Danielle D., & Deborah Dougherty. 2016. "Abductive Reasoning: How Innovators Navigate in the Labyrinth of Complex Product Innovation." *Organization Studies* 37:131–159.

20 Ibid., 146.
21 Ibid., 143.
22 Weick, Karl E. 2006. "Faith, Evidence and Action: Better Guesses in an Unknowable World." *Organization Studies* 27(11):1732.
23 Dietz, Doug. 2012. "Transforming Healthcare for Children and Their Families." *TEDxSanJoseCA*. Video. www.youtube.com/watch?v=jajduxPD6H4, accessed June 2023.
24 Bolton, Guy. 2016 (January 21). "By Turning Medical Scans into Adventures, GE Eases Children's Fears." *Milwaukee Journal Sentinel*. https://archive.jsonline. com/business/by-turning-medical-scansinto-adventures-ge-eases-childrens-fears-b99647870z1-366161191.html, accessed June 2023.
25 Ain, Aron. 2019. *Work Inspired: How to Build an Organization Where Everyone Loves to Work*. New York: McGraw-Hill.
26 Pratt, Lisa. n.d. "Disruption from within." *Washington Post*. Video. www. washingtonpost.com/brand-studio/hpe/disruption-from-within/, accessed June 2023.
27 Ain, Aron. 2019. *Work Inspired: How to Build an Organization Where Everyone Loves to Work*. New York: McGraw-Hill; Myers, Jessica. 2019. "Kronos Celebrated for Groundbreaking Cloud Transformation and Culture of Continuous Innovation." *Business Wire*. www.businesswire.com/news/home/20190910005586/en/Kronos-Celebrated-for-Groundbreaking-Cloud-Transformation-and-Culture-of-Continuous-Innovation, accessed June 2023.
28 Nadella, Satya, with Greg Shaw, & Jill Tracie Nichols. 2017. *Hit Refresh: The Quest to Rediscover Microsoft's Soul and Imagine a Better Future for Everyone*. New York: Harper Collins Publishers, p. 83.

REFERENCES

Ain, Aron. 2019. *Work Inspired: How to Build an Organization Where Everyone Loves to Work*. New York: McGraw-Hill.
Austin, Robert Daniel, Lee Devin, & E.E. Sullivan. 2012. "Accidental Innovation: Supporting Valuable Unpredictability in the Creative Process." *Organization Science* 23(5):1505–1522.
Bolton, Guy. 2016 (January 21). "By Turning Medical Scans into Adventures, GE Eases Children's Fears." *Milwaukee Journal Sentinel*. https://archive.jsonline. com/business/by-turning-medical-scansinto-adventures-ge-eases-childrens-fears-b99647870z1-366161191.html, accessed June 2023.
Cook, Scott. 2015 (November 4). "Savor the Surprises" (Presentation in a course). *Stanford eCorner*. Video. http://ecorner.stanford.edu/videos/3597/Savor-the-Surprises, accessed June 2023.
Cunha, Miguel Pinae, Stewart R. Clegg, & Ken Kamoche. 2006. "Surprises in Management and Organization: Concept, Sources, and a Typology." *British Journal of Management* 17:317–329.
Dietz, Doug. 2012. "Transforming Healthcare for Children and Their Families." *TEDxSanJoseCA*. Video. www.youtube.com/watch?v=jajduxPD6H4, accessed June 2023.

Dunne, Danielle D., & Deborah Dougherty. 2016. "Abductive Reasoning: How Innovators Navigate in the Labyrinth of Complex Product Innovation." *Organization Studies* 37:131–159.

Golden-Biddle, Karen A. 2020. "Discovery as Abductive Mechanism for Reorienting Habits within Organizational Change." *Academy of Management Journal* 63(6):1951–1975.

Kelly, David, & Tom Kelly. 2013a. "The Journey from Design Thinking to Creative Confidence. *IDEO*. Blog. www.ideou.com/blogs/inspiration/from-design-thinking-to-creative-confidence, accessed June 2023.

Kelly, David, & Tom Kelly. 2013b. *Creative Confidence: Unleashing the Creative Potential within Us All*. New York: Crown Business Publishers.

Lampel, Joseph, & Zur Shapira. 2001. "Judgmental Errors, Interactive Norms, and the Difficulty of Detecting Strategic Surprises." *Organization Science* 12(5):599–611.

Locke, Karen, Karen Golden-Biddle, & Martha S. Feldman. 2008. "Making Doubt Generative: Rethinking the Role of Doubt in the Research Process." *Organization Science* 19(6):907.

McDaniel, Reuben R., Michelle E. Jordan, & Brigitte F. Fleeman. 2003. "Surprise, Surprise, Surprise! A Complexity Science View of the Unexpected." *Health Care Management Review* 28:266–278.

Myers, Jessica. 2019. "Kronos Celebrated for Groundbreaking Cloud Transformation and Culture of Continuous Innovation." *Business Wire*. www.businesswire.com/news/home/20190910005586/en/Kronos-Celebrated-for-Groundbreaking-Cloud-Transformation-and-Culture-of-Continuous-Innovation, accessed June 2023.

Nadella, Satya, with Greg Shaw, & Jill Tracie Nichols. 2017. *Hit Refresh: The Quest to Rediscover Microsoft's Soul and Imagine a Better Future for Everyone*. New York: Harper Collins Publishers.

Ogle, Jason. 2018 (January 31). "The Life-Changing Impact of Empathy in Design." *Medium*. Blog. https://medium.com/user-defenders/the-impact-of-empathy-in-design-b55c3157d070, accessed June 2023.

Rankin, Amy, Rogier Woltjer, & Joris Field. 2016. "Sensemaking Following Surprise in the Cockpit—A Re-framing Problem." *Cognition, Technology and Work* 18:623–642.

Weick, Karl E. 2006. "Faith, Evidence and Action: Better Guesses in an Unknowable World." *Organization Studies* 27(11):1723–1736.

Winfrey, Graham. 2014 (July 25). "Intuit's Scott Cook on the Surprising Sources of Massive Growth." *Inc Magazine*. www.inc.com/graham-winfrey/intuit-s-scott-cook-on-savoring-surprises.html, accessed June 2023.

 Harnessing Genuine Doubt

Canlis, a 73-year-old, high-end Seattle restaurant,[1] was at the epicenter of the first US coronavirus outbreak. On February 29, 2020, when news came of the first confirmed US death from Covid-19 in Washington state, Mark and Brian Canlis, restaurant co-owners and brothers, started questioning what it might mean for the restaurant and staff: "It was a time of just great perception," said Mark, "trying to understand and make sense of what we were hearing. How it pertained to us and our team."[2]

On March 4, the brothers met with five senior leaders at an offsite location. They wanted to think through the situation and its implications. Tourism was down. Dinner cancellations were up. And as they were meeting, a Washington state official announced on livestream that ten people had died from Covid only five days after the first confirmed death.

"I remember watching the livestream," the owners later recalled.[3] "We're all huddled on the couch. At first, it's like the sucker punch to the system. You've got the wind taken out of you." Stung by this unexpected new reality, the brothers and their 115 employees were thrust into the realm of the unknown. Yet their story serves as an illustration not just of how to handle crisis in a pandemic, but how to handle crisis of any kind when an organization has to change its beliefs to survive.

In the words of French physiologist Claude Bernard: "Those who do not know the torment of the unknown cannot have the joy of discovery." That is, they needed to figure out how to embrace the torment of the unknown, but not let it derail them. Searching for a

DOI: 10.4324/9781003513681-5

survival strategy,[4] they weighed the daunting option of shutting down the business. They would have to cancel 1,000 reservations, which meant returning $400,000[5] to pre-paying customers. But they also questioned whether they could risk more by shuttering the business and hunkering down than if they would do something radical.

They faced a choice:[6] Would they "lean into the fear," as they said, or face the uncertainty? Said Mark, "At some point you need to . . . peer into that void of unknown and you have to courageously move forward." They couldn't let the fear suck the energy from the room. To their credit, they used it to pump up the energy. Or in the words of this book, they harnessed genuine doubt as the second motor of discovery.

My research confirms that, by harnessing genuine doubt, people raise questions in ways they never would otherwise. Facing the fear of the unknown and deciding to move forward is risky, but it positions people and organizations to know the joy of discovery. It also allows people to loosen their hold on beliefs that no longer serve them and move toward new beliefs for the future.

At Canlis, people held as a core belief—appropriate for any restaurant—that they were in the business of in-person dining. But determined not to shrink from their doubts, they now questioned this belief aloud. In light of their mission "to inspire all people to turn toward one another," they asked: What would our business look like if we were starting from scratch? Does completing our mission require that we continue as a fine-dining restaurant? What if, instead of in-person dining, we fulfill our mission by "feeding and restoring a city"?[7]

Mark recalled later[8] some additional questions: What assets are at our disposal here if we started from scratch? What are the new rules of the game? How would we play this? What do we have to be thankful for?

In struggling with these questions, the team began to gain insight into a new path forward. The new path that would move their organization into a new place to meet a new world. They would still serve customers with premium food and protect employee jobs, but they would not do it in the same way.

Emboldened by this new idea, the company's leaders announced the change to employees a few days later, emphasizing that the decision to join in was up to each employee. People were of course filled with doubt, but every one of the employees signed on. Said one senior leader, "I think that [the employee commitment to the change] was just such a boost of encouragement." He added their sentiment as leaders was simple: "If you guys are in, we're in. Let's do this."

A larger team immediately began to redesign the restaurant's operating systems. They went from the moment of shock to figuring out entirely new operations that initially supported the launch of three new pop-up businesses: a bagel shed, a drive-through burger stand, and a family meal-delivery service with a bottle of wine. The change was by no means straightforward. To operate the burger stand, they had to figure out how to serve 1,000 hamburgers a day from a kitchen that had only one fryer. Employees meanwhile shifted roles.[9] The expediter cooked bagels in the restaurant garden. Servers and pianists became delivery people.

On March 16, the day after the governor announced the temporary closure of all bars and restaurants, Canlis was ready. It had closed in-person dining and launched the new businesses with whole new operations in place to support them. In-person dining would remain closed, and it would stay that way for 471 days. But, said co-owner Brian Canlis, "they never stopped serving."[10]

Their success made Canlis a standout in the restaurant sector. That all stemmed from harnessing genuine doubt rather than rigidly adhering to the dearly held belief that they were still in the business of in-person dining.

That the company succeeded testifies to the new lease on business life that can come from harnessing doubt. It also illustrates an uncommon form of leadership. Engaging this phase paved the way for the novel shifts in belief and practice that carried them through rough times.

Most leaders don't excel at harnessing doubt so readily. They recoil at the idea of doubt because they believe that people expect them to know how to deal with new realities such as a pandemic, lackluster innovation, game-changing technology, or struggling patients, and that people expect them to know how to develop the best strategy and timing that will resolve all of these challenges.

So, too, do people make assumptions about professionals. Everyone expects accountants, lawyers, or consultants to lead the way by virtue of their expertise and guidance. Such professionals are pillars of knowledge in their discipline and share what they know with clients. They, like leaders, are viewed as trusted sources of knowledge.

Yet, professionals just about everywhere are trained to know. They are trained to understand risk. They are trained to ask tough questions. But as a result, they don't grasp one thing: They are not trained to *not know*. They are not even comfortable with not knowing. Even as the value of doubt becomes ever more essential to organizational success, they don't recognize it as a vehicle to creatively address new realities that upend prior ways of operating.

Doubt is uneasy and unsettling for everyone. What could be more human? When faced with a choice between believing and doubting, most people tend to cling tenaciously not merely to believing, but to believing only in their existing beliefs. That belief rigidity bars the path to discovery. Only through immersion in the experience of doubt, the "torment of the unknown," as Bernard said, as well as its antithesis, "the joy of discovery," can people recognize doubt as a second powerful motor of discovery.

My research confirms that when people try to block out or skip over doubt without grappling with the "torment of the unknown," they halt belief change and derail discovery. With genuine doubt as partner, however, they can imagine and develop a whole organization that experiences the "joy of discovery." That's what happened for Canlis's leaders. This helped them discover new ways of delivering fine food that were never before imagined.

In this chapter, I profile the nature of genuine doubt, the intense feelings that accompany honestly dealing with the unknown, and the tools to embrace and gain from doubt when you recognize its latent value. The road to gaining the benefits of doubt is not easy. This is when you struggle with a difficult and often troublesome choice between two directions. Do you hold onto original beliefs, clinging to believing what you believe? Or do you loosen your hold on beliefs and move to the edge of doubt's abyss? Only by grappling with the "torment" and peering into the "void" can you reap discovery's joys, helping your organization to thrive and grow.

Figure 4.1 sketches out this critical segment in your journey of discovery, coming directly after you have struggled with surprise. At the start of embracing doubt, you stand at the juncture between prevailing beliefs—knowing—and not knowing what comes next. You see, painfully so, that available beliefs and practices no longer fit the new reality. You are not able yet to ascertain where you might be headed to get to solid ground again. But by questioning your existing beliefs, by harnessing genuine doubt, you energize an imaginative search for new beliefs you can stand on.

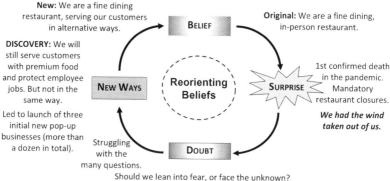

FIGURE 4.1 Redesigning core ways of operating during a crisis.

THE NATURE OF GENUINE DOUBT

The Canlis leadership team didn't let self-doubt paralyze their actions—though it easily could have if they had clung to existing beliefs and tried to hunker down long enough to re-open their in-person dining operation months later. Nor did the team take steps to eliminate doubt by denying what was happening and holding steadfast to existing beliefs. Instead, they confronted the void of the unknown head-on, not in a shallow and perfunctory way, but in a deep and sincere way. That's because the Canlis leaders faced what the pragmatism scholar Charles Peirce[11] called "genuine doubt"—doubt that interrupts the working of your beliefs.

Knowing and feeling the torment of genuine doubt is not the same as being momentarily skeptical of a belief, then searching for ways to validate it. Nor is it the same as just uttering any question and then pretending to doubt. You experience genuine doubt only when situations interrupt beliefs you've held closely that used to work well and no longer do. What used to be obvious becomes problematic. The existing beliefs cannot explain the new realities.

You can see how this happened at Canlis. So, too, can you see it in the situation that challenged industrial designer Doug Dietz in the last chapter. Dietz expected accolades for his MRI machine because he believed his design had exceeded its purpose of serving young children. After all, it was an award-winning machine. But when he saw the terror in the young girl about to undergo an MRI, his experience forced him to confront this new reality and to feel the urgent need for its resolution. His genuine doubt presented obstacles to moving forward as usual.

An experience, even small in appearance, can spark genuine doubt. It can even produce a momentary *crisis of confidence*—the feeling of having the rug pulled out from under oneself. The Canlis brothers and Dietz were on the edge of that rug but they saw the fabric of reality underneath them was moving. They had to address the void at the edge. They did not merely go through pretensions of doubt. They entered a period of limbo to loosen their hold on non-fitting beliefs and take up new, well-fitting ones.

The irony, of course, is that the discomfort of genuine doubt provides a comforting upside. By embracing it and stepping outside your comfort zone of knowing, ill-fitting beliefs come under scrutiny. The doubt spurs you to no longer assume those beliefs' validity in a new reality. The experience of genuine doubt, you realize, is a milestone on the journey of severing old beliefs and gaining new ones. The epigram on that milestone: No genuine doubting of beliefs, no discovery.

Doubtful Energy

The hidden lining of embracing doubt is that, in calling for new answers, you make new action possible. You may experience irritation with doubt, but it also moves you—maybe implores you—to find new ways to reestablish certainty and stabilize the situation. Doubt thus energizes your search to find answers to questions and gain new understanding. You bring to the fore new beliefs and never-before-considered possibilities that might fit the new reality.

The struggle to resolve genuine doubt is not effortless. Indeed, it is effortful and can bring discomfort. That's because you acknowledge and are vulnerable with others about what you don't know. You wrestle with how to proceed. You no longer defend ill-fitting beliefs, like Canlis leaders when they stopped protecting in-person, fine dining. You ask: What action could you take to yield viable new ways and end doubt?

You consider and try new beliefs and practices, then modify, transform, or abandon them, try again, and so on, until you create new ways of operating that productively resolve your genuine doubt. This is just what happened with Canlis leaders who struggled to achieve their mission in the absence of what had been their main business. And it's just what happened to Dietz, who reeled from seeing the young girl's fear of his machine. Their doubt about how they would proceed energized their search for solutions.

Neither Canlis leaders and staff nor Dietz knew that the novel solutions they created would yield success, but they were open to that uncertainty. This permissiveness allowed them to loosen constraints on their thinking. As a result, Canlis leaders' new businesses served high-quality food to nourish a city of people living and working from home. Dietz imagined GE's new "Adventure" MRI series that would bring play to children undergoing an MRI. Genuine doubt was the source of their inventiveness.

DISCOVERY ENABLERS: HARNESSING GENUINE DOUBT

John Patrick Shanley, the Pulitzer Prize–winning playwright, once said: "Certainty is a closed door. It's the end of the conversation. Doubt is an open door." If Shanley's insight has any truth to it, you would never know it in most organizations. Most people dare not go through that open door and down the dimly lit hallway into uncertainty. Leaders, in particular, focus more on getting rid of genuine doubt than on harnessing its inventive power.

Yet, genuine doubt as the second motor of discovery offers a prized vehicle for crossing into a rich landscape of potentially rewarding unknowns. It fuels novel questions. It prompts new ideas and insights. It suggests alternate paths forward—even if it doesn't feel so promising when you're feeling its heat. As you move tentatively through its door, you start to make an unsettling feeling productive. You create space for new possibilities to unfold. You tap into latent energy. Genuine doubt promises transformation.

Genuine doubt needs to be actively engaged, however. It needs to be engaged in the quiet of your office and in the company of your colleagues. Together, you have to harness it in one cycle of discovery after another to realize escalating returns in driving the creation of fundamentally new ways of operating. To engage it skillfully, my research shows you need to develop know-how in three discovery enablers: ask questions from a discovery mindset; strike a balance of belief and doubt; and deploy hypothetical entities.

Without these enablers, you and the people in your organization will remain inclined toward certainty and toward valuing the known over the unknown. But with them, you increase your receptivity to the unknown. With them, you give yourself the key to release yourself from the constraints of ill-fitting beliefs. And with them, you discover

Asking Questions From a Discovery Mindset

the capability to creatively resolve genuine doubt and stabilize the unsettled situation with new beliefs and practices.

For Charles Peirce, the "starting of any question, no matter how small or great"[12] indicates doubt. Questions signal not knowing. By contrast, answers that resolve that question indicate belief. Answers signal knowing. So, the first enabler in using doubt is to question what you "know" and then resolve your questioning to launch new ways that make new sense of the puzzling situation.

The right questions are key: Asking just any question doesn't generate doubt in a way that enables new resolutions. Sometimes people ask questions that can be disingenuous—for example, when people ask questions to which they already know the answer. Or when they ask questions, but only entertain those answers that support their particular view.

At other times, people ask sincere questions, but ones designed to validate a belief, not harness doubt. That can happen when people seek to confirm observations too early, when what is needed instead is further discovery. The Centers for Disease Control and Prevention (CDC) misdiagnosed a 1999 West Nile virus outbreak in New York City as St. Louis encephalitis (SLE).[13] For many reasons, it took three weeks to catch the error, but one was the designation of the CDC as a testing laboratory. This designation meant that instead of expecting to not know what the sample tests would reveal, they "looked specifically for what they presumed they would find, namely, SLE."[14] They asked a question with a confirmation mindset. That is, they wanted to know, "Is SLE in this sample?" They neglected to ask questions from a discovery mindset, such as "What do we face here?" That question could have led to recognition that SLE was only one possibility. In the end, it took others to harness genuine doubt and correct the original SLE diagnosis.

When you go about harnessing doubt, the permissiveness of the questions themselves—generated with discovery's logic of hunches and conjectures—encourages you to seek answers to what is *not known*. They also prompt you to consider, *if it were known*, how this new understanding would challenge existing beliefs.

Centuries ago, the Greek philosopher Socrates encouraged questions from a discovery mindset. Through his efforts, he taught people how to think critically by asking questions that shed light on the principles, beliefs, and assumptions that underlaid their own and others' thinking. Similarly, asking questions from a discovery mindset allows you to loosen constraints on your thinking and your hold on ill-fitting beliefs. Such questioning opens, rather than shuts, doors to the unknown. It affirms rather than ignores uncertainties. It generates feelings of irritation that motivate your search for answers.

Questions from a discovery mindset also recognize that people, together, generate knowledge during the process of harnessing doubt. Knowledge is not something individuals possess beforehand. Everyone must discover and make sense of the new knowledge together. The benefits of asking questions to harness genuine doubt come to the organization as a whole.

Striking a Balance of Belief and Doubt

How do you embrace genuine doubt?

You certainly don't want to fall into the trap pointed out by Henri Poincaré, the French polymath: "To doubt everything and to believe everything are two equally convenient solutions; each saves us from thinking." On the one hand, if you ignore questions and uncertainties, believing everything, you can become overconfident and certain in what you know. You stop searching for what is not known. And as a leader, you create a rigid culture of belief with minimal doubting. On the other hand, if you ignore answers and certainties, doubting everything, you can become overly cautious and cynical, not trusting what you do know. You stop searching for what is known, and you create a chaotic culture of doubt with minimal knowing.

Instead, you need to have confidence in what you do know but also treat what you know cautiously, even as potentially in error.[15] You need to hold your beliefs with flexibility, not rigidity. You need to argue as if you are right, while listening as if you are wrong.[16] Paradoxically, you need to believe and to doubt—at the same time! When you do that, you keep your belief rigidity in check and harness the power of genuine doubt to spur discovery.

A key enabler of discovery is striking a balance of belief and doubt. That means that you don't let excesses of either belief or doubt persist. You don't exude too much or too little knowing. You don't, in other words, set yourself, team, and organization up for suppressing discovery. Instead, you practice both belief *and* doubt.

Learn-it-all cultures, such as the ones in Microsoft and Canlis, strike a balance of belief and doubt by ingraining flexibility of belief and supporting people's efforts to harness genuine doubt. Such simultaneous believing and doubting helps you be less committed to justifying current ways of operating and more committed to reorienting them in light of new realities. You win at discovery by cultivating a creative context of ambivalence.[17]

Injecting Doubt to Mitigate Overconfidence

As a part of striking the right balance, you want to avoid what American historian Daniel Boorstin[18] called the "greatest obstacle to discovery: the 'illusion of knowledge.'" It's too easy to overemphasize what you think you know, while failing to recognize the inherent *fallibility* of that knowing. You may hold flawed beliefs without realizing it.[19]

Instead, you want to inject just enough doubt into your work to mitigate overconfidence. If you do so, you and your colleagues won't be held captive by your overconfidence and, in turn, dismiss doubt and suppress discovery. This prepares you to adjust course when encountering unexpected new realities. You raise the process of discovery to a new level.

The story of physicians and administrators in British Royal Infirmary from chapter 1 shows the importance for discovery of avoiding overconfidence in flawed beliefs. These healthcare experts were unable to treat their explanation for poor surgery performance as fallible knowledge. They refused to consider alternate explanations. Their overconfidence in what they knew, fueled by belief rigidity, prevented them from harnessing doubt and generating insight that could have helped them correct their errors.

EXPLICITLY CONSIDERING UNKNOWNS

One simple tool for injecting doubt to mitigate overconfidence is to ask people to list what they don't know as part of projects or other initiatives. Three experimental studies by university researchers Daniel Walters, Philip Fernbach, Craig Fox, and Steven Sloman[20] provide support for this action. In the first study, they asked participants to complete two-alternative, forced-choice trivia questions and judge the probability that their answers were correct. In their subsequent studies, they asked participants to list their unknowns prior to assessing the probability of correct answers.

The studies found that overconfidence was driven in the first study by participants failing to incorporate unknown variables as they answered the questions. Then, when participants were later asked to list their unknowns in advance, drawing attention to unknowns reduced their confidence in those areas of overconfidence. Said the researchers, "People tend to underappreciate what they don't know. Thus, overconfidence is driven in part by insufficient consideration of unknown evidence."[21]

SAYING "I DON'T KNOW" HONESTLY

Another way of injecting doubt is to make a point of saying that you don't know. Admitting you don't know is not the same as admitting ignorance, though that is often the presumption. When you are direct about what you don't know, you and your team still have confidence in what you do know. To be sure, making yourself vulnerable in this way can be difficult. Even when you know that you don't know how to proceed, you may feel exposed to criticism. But, James Whitehurst, former President of IBM, and former CEO of open-source software maker Red Hat, notes his different experience: "Being very open about the things I did not know actually had the opposite effect than I would have thought. It helped me build credibility."[22]

CREATING A LEARNING CULTURE ORIENTED TO DISCOVERY

A third way to inject doubt to mitigate overconfidence is to create a culture that values the unknown—what I call a learning culture with a discovery orientation. Professor Uri Alon, a cell biologist at the Weizmann Institute in Israel, created such a culture in his laboratory. I first learned about his work a few years ago from a doctoral student taking my class, who shared the link to his TED Talk, found in the endnotes.[23]

In his lab, members learn that research is not a straight line from question to answer. To discover something new, they and he must face the unknown. Alon calls this place the "cloud," which stands at the threshold between the known and the unknown. Embracing the cloud is essential because "in order to discover something truly new, at least one of your basic assumptions has to change." He describes this cloud as a place where "experiments don't work, experiments don't work, experiments don't work, until you reach a place linked with negative emotions where it seems like your basic assumptions have stopped making sense, like somebody yanked the carpet beneath your feet."

In valuing the cloud, Alon has normalized genuine doubt in his lab. This is critical because research shows that fear closes down your mind's ways of thinking. He explains that if you want to engage genuine doubt, you need other emotions such as "solidarity, support, hope that come with your connection from somebody else, so . . . it's best to walk into the unknown together."

Injecting Belief to Mitigate Debilitating Doubt

By contrast, when excesses of doubt persist, people become too cautious. The result? They are held captive by debilitating doubt. Instead of embracing what is known, they focus instead on all the uncertainties, puzzles, and unknowns. In contrast to dismissing the *fallibility* of knowing, with debilitating doubt, they dismiss the *knowing*. Without belief as a guide, excess caution freezes action. People experience paralysis.

DOUBTING YOUR TOOLS, NOT YOURSELF

Perhaps the most pernicious form of this paralysis is self-doubt. For a long time, researchers regarded self-doubt solely as a negative phenomenon. It occurred when people focused on their shortcomings so much that they became overwhelmed by doubt. At its worst, they were consumed by it.

But more recently, researchers find benefits of self-doubt when distinguishing between doubting your ideas or tools and doubting yourself. For example, artists may doubt their ideas but then get absorbed in debilitating doubt about themselves. Patrick Carroll, professor at Ohio State University explains: "They can't get past that phase of self-doubt. They go from, 'I don't know about this idea' to 'I don't know about myself' and they get stuck there."[24]

In his book *Think Again*, organizational psychologist and Wharton professor Adam Grant[25] provides further support for the distinction. Confidence—a measure of your belief in yourself—is distinct from competence—a measure of your belief in your ideas, tools, and methods. Grant developed a helpful diagnostic that differentiates the conditions of each, shown in Figure 4.2.

Debilitating self-doubt can get the better of you when you are insecure in beliefs about yourself (confidence) and uncertain in your beliefs about your tools (competence). Overconfidence, or "blind arrogance," is the opposite of debilitating self-doubt. You are secure about your beliefs in yourself and certain about your beliefs in your tools. The sweet spot is of course confident humility—or, in the words of this chapter, when you strike a balance between belief and doubt. You are secure in your beliefs about yourself and can be uncertain about your beliefs in your tools.

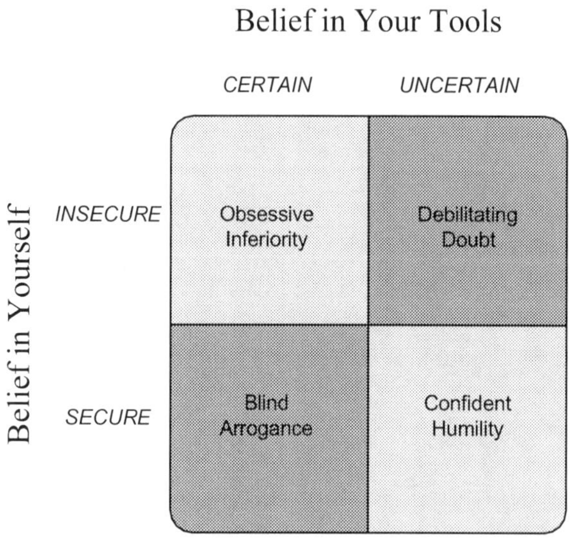

Belief in Your Tools

	CERTAIN	UNCERTAIN
INSECURE	Obsessive Inferiority	Debilitating Doubt
SECURE	Blind Arrogance	Confident Humility

Belief in Yourself

FIGURE 4.2 The Confidence Sweet Spot from *Think Again: The Power of Knowing What You Don't Know* by Adam Grant, copyright© 2021 by Adam Grant.

Source: Used by permission of Viking Books, an imprint of Penguin Publishing Group, a division of Penguin Random House LLC. All rights reserved.

GENERATING SMALL WINS

The strategy of seeking small wins is especially effective in righting the course of discovery in contexts of excess doubt.[26] Small wins increase confidence, critical for injecting belief that mitigates too much doubt. This was the case in Canlis when the leaders saw the early results of their initial three pop-up businesses in light of the new reality. These wins injected belief into the overly cautious present, which increased their confidence and facilitated a shift in their attention toward organizing these desired future possibilities. Research on the use of small wins in organizations[27] finds similar effects, including increased confidence in legitimizing a new role, positive impact on people's feelings about progress in project work, and momentum to reduce long waits in a medical center emergency department.

INVOKING MEANINGFUL MISSION, PURPOSE, VALUES

A final way to mitigate too much doubt and strike a balance between belief and doubt is to keep the focus on the mission, purpose, and values. By many accounts, Canlis was the first restaurant to "pivot" operations during the pandemic, getting media credit for the new ideas and businesses spawned.[28] Yet, when discussing the pivot, the Canlis brothers focused instead on the process of pivoting, not its outcome in the restaurant business.[29] Mark and Brian explained later that the part of their operations that shifted got all the credit for yielding something new. But for them, the more stable part deserved the credit for enabling the shift. "We all agreed," the brothers explained, "that our planted foot, our mission statement foot, our values foot, [was] the magic of the pivot—placing your weight or the significance of who you are in the right spot."

Using the beliefs embedded in the mission and values generated confidence among their leadership team and employees. This helped mitigate the excess doubt over the "void of the unknown." Just like basketball players, they planted their stable foot to give them the power to shed the ill-fitting belief of in-person dining while swinging the rest of their corporate body to face and adopt new beliefs and practices. In balancing belief and doubt, they gained confidence and the momentum for further discovery.

Deploying Hypothetical Entities

The third enabler of discovery in harnessing genuine doubt is the deployment of hypothetical entities. These entities are managerial plans, rules, prototyping, what-if scenarios, drawings, goals, specialized vocabularies, budgets, and more that offer suggested or conjectural ways forward. They are vehicles that people use to navigate between their present situation and a future one. Using hypothetical entities helps people step back from their experience, creating the opportunity to reflect on their present situation and how it might transition to a future one.

The initial entity used by Canlis's leadership was a powerful what-if and as-if question: If they were to "feed and restore a city," what would that look like if they were starting from scratch? This hypothetical entity got them to start writing a new story of their business that began with how they would go about fulfilling their mission "to inspire all people to turn toward one another," as if they were starting over. It subsequently supported more than a dozen other entities, or configurations, each one conveying new, immediate-future possibilities for action, initially including the bagel shed, the drive-through hamburger stand, and the family meal-delivery service. Together, the three initial and subsequent entities represented heretofore unimagined initiatives that would help them reorient their beliefs and practices to meet the highly disrupted, unsettled situation.

As a caution, the use of hypothetical entities often fails to harness doubt because people use them to codify present beliefs to sustain present situations rather than questioning them. This often happens because people either forget about the puzzles, clues, or surprises that prompted their use in the first place, or they seek to maintain the current situation. This happens even with prototypes, a prevalent device used explicitly to produce something new.

Paul Leonardi, professor at the University of California, Santa Barbara,[30] has found that many companies move prototyping too quickly from their original "quick-and-dirty" form to a more detailed, "polished" form. At one automaker, Leonardi's research showed that the rapid shift to polished form redirected the team's attention away from brainstorming. That led the team to overlook "any remaining ambiguities about the problem the product is meant to solve."[31] In effect, they derailed any subsequent exploration of what they didn't know.

By removing the ambiguities elicited by doubt from their deliberations so early, the team generated false confidence in the prototype as complete. Leonardi proposes instead that organizations hold the ambiguity longer and move on only after the team gains clarity on the problems meant to be solved. Retaining ambiguity brings knowing and not-knowing back into balance.

Despite the risks, the intentional use of hypothetical entities is critical for harnessing doubt because they stimulate curiosity and creativity. Unlike the team using prototypes, the trick is to treat the entities as tentative or provisional, building them from acts such as guesses, hunches, working hypotheses, or configurations about the present doubtful situation. You and your team shape these entities by generating insight, new ideas, and perspectives about them over time. By treating these entities as provisional, you leave open the door to additional surprises and discoveries throughout your work with them.

SUMMARY

In all of our interactions with experience—physical and mental—we must make two kinds of choices in the face of genuine doubt. One involves the application of our existing beliefs to the puzzling situation that might open up genuine doubt. The other choice involves the generation of new beliefs and practices that might resolve our genuine doubt. With each step into doubt, you risk the torment of the unknown but gain the capability to experience the joy of discovery.

Although surprise and genuine doubt are critical and necessary motors, one more motor yields important benefits of discovery. You need to launch new ways, the subject of the next chapter. More than experimentation, this third motor involves your experience-driven search for new beliefs and practices to resolve the puzzling situation. When you enact all three motors, you embrace the discovery process to generate viable new ways that stabilize the original situation and create desired futures.

~~~~~

1. Think of a situation when you didn't know something that you believed you should have known. What feelings and thoughts did you encounter in your experience of *not knowing*? Which discovery enablers in this chapter could have helped you deal with the situation?
2. Imagine that a friend has shared her self-doubt with you. How could you use the ideas from this chapter to help her?
3. Write down a question developed from a discovery mindset. Then, write that same question from a discovery *suppression* mindset. Repeat this one more time, with a different question. What differentiates the questions written from a discovery versus a suppression mindset?

NOTES

1 Canlis was founded in 1950 in Seattle. At the time of this writing, it is 73 years old.
2 Gilbert, Ben, & David Rosenthal. 2020 (March 20). "Canlis: Episode 1." Adapting (by Acquired) Podcast. www.youtube.com/watch?app=desk top&v=EVr4bWy0f7s, accessed June 2023. See also: Loh, Stefanie, & Jackie Variano. 2020 (March 12). Updated March 26, 2020. "Amid Coronavirus Outbreak, Seattle's Canlis Halts Dining Room Service to Start Drive-Thru and Delivery Services." *Seattle Times*. www.seattle times.com/life/food-drink/seattles-canlis-to-temporarily-halt-dining-room-service-amid-coronavirus-outbreak/, accessed June 2023.
3 Gilbert, Ben, & David Rosenthal. 2020 (March 20). "Canlis: Episode 1." Adapting (by Acquired) Podcast. www.youtube.com/watch?app=desk

top&v=EVr4bWy0f7s, accessed June 2023. See also: Lee, Wilson K., with Mark Canlis. 2020 (April 23). "How Top Fine Dining Restaurant Is Adapting to COVID-19." Restaurant Management Podcast. www.youtube.com/watch?v=P2G0iKaJwxY, accessed June 2023.
4. Smith, Lilly. 2020 (March 16). "This Seattle Restaurant Is Redesigning Its Entire Business Model in Response to the Coronavirus." *Fast Company*. www.fastcompany.com/90477161/this-seattle-restaurant-is-redesigning-its-entire-business-model-in-response-to-coronavirus, accessed June 2023.
5. Walsh, Kate, with Mark & Brian Canlis. "Reframing and Innovating Through the Pandemic: The Story of the Canlis Brothers." *Cornell University*. Interview. https:// ecornell.cornell.edu/keynotes/view/K020221/, accessed June 2023.
6. Gilbert, Ben, & David Rosenthal. 2020 (March 20). "Canlis: Episode 1." Adapting (by Acquired) Podcast. www.youtube.com/watch?app=desktop&v=EVr4bWy0f7s, accessed June 2023. See also: Loh, Stefanie, & Jackie Variano. 2020 (March 12). Updated March 26, 2020. "Amid Coronavirus Outbreak, Seattle's Canlis Halts Dining Room Service to Start Drive-Thru and Delivery Services." *Seattle Times*. www. seattletimes.com/life/food-drink/seattles-canlis-to-temporarily-halt-dining-room-service-amid-coronavirus-outbreak/, accessed June 2023.
7. Smith, Lilly. 2020 (March 16). "This Seattle Restaurant Is Redesigning Its Entire Business Model in Response to the Coronavirus." *Fast Company*. www.fastcompany. com/90477161/this-seattle-restaurant-is-redesigning-its-entire-business-model-in-response-to-coronavirus, accessed June 2023.
8. Lee, Wilson K., with Mark Canlis. 2020 (April 23). "How Top Fine Dining Restaurant Is Adapting to COVID-19." Restaurant Management Podcast. www.youtube.com/watch?v=P2G0iKaJwxY, accessed June 2023.
9. Smith, Lilly. 2020 (March 16). "This Seattle Restaurant Is Redesigning Its Entire Business Model in Response to the Coronavirus." *Fast Company*. www.fastcompany. com/90477161/this-seattle-restaurant-is-redesigning-its-entire-business-model-in-response-to-coronavirus, accessed June 2023. See also: Gordinier, Jeff. 2020 (March 18). "Before Coronavirus, Canlis Was the Epitome of Fine Dining. Now, It's a Damn-Good Drive-Thru." *Esquire*. www.esquire.com/food-drink/restaurants/a31709260/canlis-seattle-coronavirus-restaurant-takeout-solution/, accessed June 2023.
10. Walsh, Kate, with Mark & Brian Canlis. "Reframing and Innovating Through the Pandemic: The Story of the Canlis Brothers." *Cornell University*. Interview. https:// ecornell.cornell.edu/keynotes/view/K020221/, accessed June 2023.
11. Peirce, Charles Sanders. 1955. "What Pragmatism Is." In *Philosophical Writings of Peirce*. Edited by J. Buchler. New York: Dover Publications, pp. 266–267.
12. Peirce, Charles Sanders. 1878. "Illustrations of the Logic of Science: How to Make Our Ideas Clear." *Popular Science Monthly* 1&2 (January).
13. Adapted from Weick, Karl E. 2002. "Puzzles in Organizational Learning: An Exercise in Disciplined Imagination." *British Journal of Management* 13:S7–S15.

14 Ibid., S14.
15 Meacham, Jack A. 1990. "The Loss of Wisdom." In *Metaphors of Mind: Conceptions of the Nature of Intelligence*. Edited by Robert J. Sternberg. Cambridge. U.K: Cambridge University Press, pp. 181–211, p. 182.
16 Sutton, Robert I. 2010 (July 15). "A Great Boss Is Confident, But Not Really Sure." *Harvard Business Review*. https://hbr.org/2010/07/confident-but-not-really-sure, accessed June 2023.
17 Rothman, Naomi B., Brianna B. Caza, Shimul Melwani, & Kate Walsh. 2021 (September 14). "Embracing the Power of Ambivalence." *Harvard Business Review*. https://hbr.org/2021/09/embracing-the-power-of-ambivalence, accessed June 2023.
18 Kruckoff, Carol. 1984 (January 29). "The 6 O'Clock Scholar: Librarian of Congress Daniel Boorstin and His Love Affair with Books." *The Washington Post*. www.washingtonpost.com/archive/lifestyle/1984/01/29/the-6-oclock-scholar/eed58de4-2dcb-47d2-8947-b0817a18d8fe/, accessed June 2023.
19 This may not be as surprising as it seems due to the Dunning-Kruger effect. This cognitive bias occurs when people lack knowledge and skills in certain areas but overestimate their competence in that area. When lacking competence, people may become overconfident and not know they hold this bias.
20 Walters, Daniel J., P.M. Fernbach, Craig R. Fox, & S.A. Sloman. 2017. "Known Unknowns: A Critical Determinant of Confidence and Calibration." *Management Science* 63(12):4298–4307.
21 Ibid., 4305.
22 Zak, Paul J. 2017. "The Neuroscience of Trust." *Harvard Business Review* (January–February):90.
23 Alon, Uri. 2013."Why Science Demands a Leap into the Unknown." *TED Global*. Video. www.ted.com/talks/uri_alon_why_science_demands_a_leap_into_the_unknown, accessed June 2023.
24 Carroll, Patrick J., R.M. Arkin, & C.K. Shade. 2011. "Possible Selves and Self-Doubt: A Poverty of Desired Possibility." *Social Psychological and Personality Science* 2(2):190–198.
25 Grant, Adam. 2021. *Think Again: The Power of Knowing What You Don't Know*. New York: Viking.
26 Small wins are opportunities that are doable, controllable, modest in size, and produce visible results.
27 See: Amabile, Teresa M., & S.J. Kramer. 2011. "The Power of Small Wins." *Harvard Business Review* 89(5):70–81. See also: Arbune, Amit, Sarah Wackerbarth, Penne Allison, & Joseph Conigliaro. 2017. "Improvement Through Small Cycles of Change: Lessons from an Academic Medical Center Emergency Department." *Journal for Healthcare Quality* 1 (September). And Reay, T., Karen Golden-Biddle, & K. GermAnn, 2006. "Legitimizing a New Role: Small Wins and Microprocesses of Change." *Academy of Management Journal* 49(5):977–998.
28 Anderson, Brett. 2020 (October 13). Updated October 16, 2020. "The News Cycle Is Crushing Seattle's Vibrant Restaurant Scene." *The New York Times*. www.nytimes.com/2020/10/13/dining/seattle-restaurants-coronavirus.html, accessed June 2023.
29 Walsh, Kate, with Mark & Brian Canlis. "Reframing and Innovating Through the Pandemic: The Story of the Canlis Brothers." *Cornell Uni-*

versity. Interview. https:// ecornell.cornell.edu/keynotes/view/K020221/, accessed June 2023.

30 Leonardi, Paul M. 2011. "Innovation Blindness: Culture, Frames, and Cross-Boundary Problem Construction in the Development of New Technology Concepts." *Organization Science* 22(2):347–369. See also: Leonardi, Paul M. 2011. "Early Prototypes Can Hurt a Team's Creativity." *Harvard Business Review* (December):28.

31 Leonardi, Paul M. 2011. "Early Prototypes Can Hurt a Team's Creativity." *Harvard Business Review* (December):28.

REFERENCES

Alon, Uri. 2013. "Why Science Demands a Leap into the Unknown." *TED Global.* Video. www.ted.com/talks/uri_alon_why_science_demands_a_leap_into_the_unknown, accessed June 2023.

Amabile, Teresa M., & S.J. Kramer. 2011. "The Power of Small Wins." *Harvard Business Review* 89(5):70–81.

Anderson, Brett. 2020 (October 13). Updated October 16, 2020. "The News Cycle Is Crushing Seattle's Vibrant Restaurant Scene." *The New York Times.* www.nytimes. com/2020/10/13/dining/seattle-restaurants-coronavirus.html, accessed June 2023.

Arbune, Amit, Sarah Wackerbarth, Penne Allison, & Joseph Conigliaro. 2017. "Improvement Through Small Cycles of Change: Lessons from an Academic Medical Center Emergency Department." *Journal for Healthcare Quality* (September/October) 39(5):259–269.

Carroll, Patrick J., R.M. Arkin, & C.K. Shade. 2011. "Possible Selves and Self-Doubt: A Poverty of Desired Possibility." *Social Psychological and Personality Science* 2(2):190–198.

Gilbert, Ben, & David Rosenthal. 2020 (March 20). "Canlis: Episode 1." Adapting (by Acquired) Podcast. www.youtube.com/watch?app=desktop&v=EVr4bWy0f7s, accessed June 2023.

Gordinier, Jeff. 2020 (March 18). "Before Coronavirus, Canlis Was the Epitome of Fine Dining. Now, It's a Damn-Good Drive-Thru." *Esquire.* www.esquire.com/food-drink/restaurants/a31709260/canlis-seattle-coronavirus-restaurant-takeout-solution/, accessed June 2023.

Grant, Adam. 2021. *Think Again: The Power of Knowing What You Don't Know.* New York: Viking.

Kruckoff, Carol. 1984 (January 29). "The 6 O'Clock Scholar: Librarian of Congress Daniel Boorstin and His Love Affair with Books." *The Washington Post.* www. washingtonpost.com/archive/lifestyle/1984/01/29/the-6-oclock-scholar/eed58de4-2dcb-47d2-8947-b0817a18d8fe/, accessed June 2023.

Lee, Wilson K., with Mark Canlis. 2020 (April 23). "How Top Fine Dining Restaurant Is Adapting to COVID-19." Restaurant Management Podcast. www.youtube.com/ watch?v=P2G0iKaJwxY, accessed June 2023.

Leonardi, Paul M. 2011a. "Early Prototypes Can Hurt a Team's Creativity." *Harvard Business Review* (December):28.

Leonardi, Paul M. 2011b. "Innovation Blindness: Culture, Frames, and Cross-Boundary Problem Construction in the Development of New Technology Concepts." *Organization Science* 22(2):347–369.

Loh, Stefanie, & Jackie Varriano. 2020 (March 12). Updated March 26, 2020. "Amid Coronavirus Outbreak, Seattle's Canlis Halts Dining Room Service to Start Drive-Thru and Delivery Services." *Seattle Times*. www.seattletimes.com/life/food-drink/seattles-canlis-to-temporarily-halt-dining-room-service-amid-coronavirus-outbreak/, accessed June 2023.

Meacham, Jack A. 1990. "The Loss of Wisdom." In *Metaphors of Mind: Conceptions of the Nature of Intelligence*. Edited by Robert J. Sternberg. Cambridge, U.K: Cambridge University Press, pp. 181–211.

Peirce, Charles Sanders. 1878. "Illustrations of the Logic of Science: How to Make Our Ideas Clear." *Popular Science Monthly* 1&2(January).

Peirce, Charles Sanders. 1955. "What Pragmatism Is." In *Philosophical Writings of Peirce*. Edited by J. Buchler. New York: Dover Publications, pp. 266–267.

Reay, T., Karen Golden-Biddle, & K. GermAnn, 2006. "Legitimizing a New Role: Small Wins and Microprocesses of Change." *Academy of Management Journal* 49(5):977–998.

Rothman, Naomi B., Brianna B. Caza, Shimul Melwani, & Kate Walsh. 2021 (September 14). "Embracing the Power of Ambivalence." *Harvard Business Review*. https://hbr.org/2021/09/embracing-the-power-of-ambivalence, accessed June 2023.

Smith, Lilly. 2020 (March 16). "This Seattle Restaurant Is Redesigning Its Entire Business Model in Response to the Coronavirus." *Fast Company*. www.fastcompany.com/90477161/this-seattle-restaurant-is-redesigning-its-entire-business-model-in-response-to-coronavirus, accessed June 2023.

Sutton, Robert I. 2010 (July 15). "A Great Boss Is Confident, But Not Really Sure." *Harvard Business Review*. https://hbr.org/2010/07/confident-but-not-really-sure, accessed June 2023.

Walsh, Kate, with Mark & Brian Canlis. "Reframing and Innovating Through the Pandemic: The Story of the Canlis Brothers." *Cornell University*. Interview. https://ecornell.cornell.edu/keynotes/view/K020221/, accessed June 2023.

Walters, Daniel J., P.M. Fernbach, Craig R. Fox, & S.A. Sloman. 2017. "Known Unknowns: A Critical Determinant of Confidence and Calibration." *Management Science* 63(12):4298–4307.

Weick, Karl E. 2002. "Puzzles in Organizational Learning: An Exercise in Disciplined Imagination." *British Journal of Management* 13:S7–S15.

Zak, Paul J. 2017. "The Neuroscience of Trust." *Harvard Business Review* (January–February): 85–90.

Launching New Ways

After completing seven years of medical school and residency for a career in oncology, Jim O'Connell (MD) thought his training was "finally over." He was on his way to serve for a year as a physician at Pine Street Inn, the largest of the health clinics serving the homeless that had been established in 1985 by the Boston Health Care for the Homeless Program. What he didn't know was that he was also on his way for yet more training. "[My] education in homelessness and poverty was just beginning,"[1] he recalls.

On his first day, O'Connell remembered thinking that as a doctor, he would be "cherished." Instead, he "walked right smack into the nurses' clinic" and nurse Barbara McInnis, who gave him the 'riot act,' as only nurses can do." She sat him down and reminded him that they had succeeded for years without help from hospitals or doctors. If he wanted to learn the work, she said, he "would do well to just watch."

O'Connell was in for an accelerated course in launching new ways: the third motor of discovery. He began the course, mentored by McInnis, as an apprentice in soaking guests' feet. "[She] took away my stethoscope," he recalls, and she told him, "You have to stop thinking like a doctor. This is not about doctoring. This is about getting to know people."

O'Connell was "devastated" yet "determined." After all his training, he was once again a trainee. Not one to reject a challenge to his authority, however, he took his cue from McInnis. He started soaking feet, and that's when he discovered that a new practice, one he ordinarily would have rejected, helped him in two respects: It challenged

DOI: 10.4324/9781003513681-6

his current beliefs about being a doctor, and it showed the pathway to new ones.

"It was quite extraordinary, because [the work] . . . puts you at the feet of the person that you're taking care of, and it respects their personal space." The beliefs he had learned as part of the Boston medical community didn't seem to fit at Pine Street. He could no longer rely on them as touchstones in one of the world's most storied cities for medical care.

The experience transformed O'Connell's way of being a doctor. In trying out a non-conventional medical practice, he discovered a new way to serve the homeless population. Would these new beliefs—beliefs at variance with the medical community around him—work in actual practice? Would they catalyze new ways to treat people? Would they produce the desired, better clinical care?

That remained to be seen. To begin with, he dedicated himself to the apprenticeship, "learning to just soak feet and say hello to people." At first, some people spoke to him, but others didn't. With time, however, most people began to speak to him. Then he began to understand the wisdom of the nurses' guidance. "I had to be present," he explained. "I had to be consistent . . . then people opened up."

Years later, O'Connell reflected on his initiation to homeless care by McInnis. He could see now that the practice of soaking feet was her way of helping him reorient his beliefs about medical treatment. Success didn't come the traditional way doctors are trained. It didn't come after patients visited the doctor. It came from the reverse. "You have to find ways to break in," he says. "When you see somebody outside, you get them a cup of coffee and sit with them." It could take up to a year before they would talk to O'Connell. But when they did, he says, "they'll come to you any time because they trust you . . . It's all about listening and patience and realizing that you don't have much control over the situation. You can serve, but you can't control."

Launching new ways, the third motor of discovery, reveals in even greater light how new perspectives and understanding make novel solutions not only possible but viable. If embracing the first motor of surprise draws people's attention to the new reality, and if harnessing the second motor of genuine doubt challenges people to acknowledge what they don't know about it, then launching new ways propels everyone to come to know the reoriented beliefs and practices that enable transformation.

O'Connell certainly encountered the surprise of a new reality. Losing his stethoscope and soaking feet got his attention fast. Sticking to it turned uncertainty into genuine doubt, which provoked agonizing questions. These, in turn, challenged prevailing beliefs in the medical community about what it meant to be a doctor and how to treat patients. As O'Connell regained his footing as a caregiver, he could shed ill-fitting beliefs and take up new ones. His work on the ground, face-to-face with a new reality, steadily positioned himself to transform the practice of medicine to better serve the homeless population.

Chief among the new beliefs required for success was the value of being "present" and "consistent"—listening, not telling people what to do. This meant getting comfortable with uncertainty and lack of control. He could not have migrated his practice to building on those new beliefs without genuinely engaging in the discovery process—and turning a nebulous, confusing situation into a coherent, desired one that better fit the future of medical care.

The story of O'Connell, in league with McInnis and other nurses at Pine Street Inn, portrays how all people can move the beliefs in their field along the arc of discovery, from questioning prior beliefs to generating and launching new ones. The process concludes with propelling action that gives form to the novel solutions based on reoriented beliefs.

In this chapter, I profile the driving force of launching new ways: situated action. To embark upon novel solutions that remake unsettled situations into desired, more stable ones, you have to act.

Your action also has to take place in, or closely simulate, the context of implementation. That's what distinguishes situated action from lab experiments and rapid prototyping in which researchers and designers remain isolated from on-the-ground struggles of dealing with the new reality. This is also the case for decision makers who, in strategizing meetings for change, all too often deliberate far from the front lines and the people impacted. By contrast, launching new ways takes place locally—in situ—on the front lines and with the people impacted.

Being immersed in the particular situation enables you and your colleagues to do the nitty-gritty work of assessing the fit of proposed new ways. O'Connell's experience highlights this aspect. He worked in a "reversed" position of power: the doctor soaking patients' feet. This enabled him to discover insights that helped him reorient the identity of doctor that he had learned in training. Discovery in situ was the key.

THE NATURE OF LAUNCHING NEW WAYS

The power of situated action is that it encourages you to discard some sets of beliefs and practices in favor of others that begin to feel more right. Your personal immersion in the context of the unsettled situation or new reality gives you direct feedback on whether or not the proposed new ways resolve the questions and irritation of genuine doubt. The immersion also helps you refine new ways and add a concreteness that enables you to assess their suitability for a particular situation or purpose. This segment in your journey of discovery is shown in Figure 5.1.

As the provisional set of practices and beliefs shows its fittingness, your irritation from doubt recedes and is replaced by feelings of confidence, as well as feelings of anticipation and excitement for what is to come. That allows you and your colleagues to make a commitment to act on new possibilities that will reorient and stabilize the situation—and may also transform yourself.

That's what happened for O'Connell, when he compared the old way of doctor training with the new way impelled by McInnis and nursing staff at the Pine Street Inn. At the beginning, his new beliefs took only general shape: Doctoring for people who are homeless meant caring for them by *not* leading with traditional medical treatment.

The same sequence of discovery happened at Canlis, in the last chapter. With nervous confidence, the team built on the provisional new belief in feeding and serving a city *without* personal contact. Likewise for Doug Dietz, in chapter three. With renewed hope, he built on the provisional new belief in designing an experience for

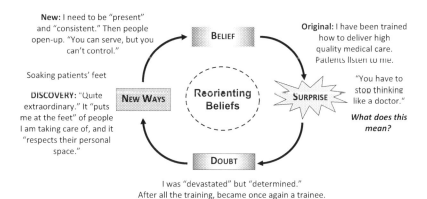

FIGURE 5.1 Rethinking what it means to be a doctor.

children undergoing MRIs that would *no longer* prioritize technological mastery over patient comfort.

The magic in launching new ways is that in participating, listening, seeing, and feeling the performance of the new ways in context, they come into sharper focus. You gain insight into their fit and suitability for your particular situation. You feel hopeful, even if you are hesitant about what is to come. You and your colleagues wonder: If you moved from surfacing novel beliefs and practices to embracing and acting on them, would they help you create a desired new situation that would remake the unsettled one?

DISCOVERY ENABLERS: LAUNCHING NEW WAYS

You can think of launching new ways, the third motor of discovery, as a vehicle for turning vague, yet promising new possibilities into suitable new ways of operating. This enabler helps you discover novel answers that resolve the questions of your doubt. You shift to being receptive, if cautious. You feel energy and hope—even while you still experience some discomfort with the new ways you and your colleagues are proposing.

To get the most out of this motor, research shows you need to develop three discovery enablers: seeing beyond your expectations, permitting recombination, and assessing suitability of new ways. When used consistently, these enablers build your capacity for closing the cycle of discovery. Although these enablers can be used together or separately, they share four important discovery-oriented features.

First, each discovery enabler *orients action so as to break through prior beliefs*. You and your colleagues make visible the contrast between old and new beliefs, between ill-fitting ones and new ones that hold the potential to restabilize the challenging situation facing you.

Second, each discovery enabler *fosters purposeful and situated action*. You and your colleagues come to care enough about this challenging situation to want to make it better through change. Your action is situated—not isolated or context-free—and is guided by your purpose in creating suitable new solutions that remake unsettled situations.

Third, each discovery enabler *acts powerfully to reorient beliefs by connecting your action and reflection*. You and your colleagues embrace new beliefs through an iterative course of acting and reflecting on the needs and challenges of the particular situation. You begin to have hope that you are building the know-how to transform how things currently operate.

Finally, each discovery enabler *requires a community* broad enough to address the unsettled situation. Together, you and your colleagues provisionally launch and, when suitable, commit to a set of beliefs and practices that you believe best resolves genuine doubt. The test of the effectiveness of the chosen new ways is the community's judgement about progress toward a new, satisfactory situation.

Seeing Beyond Your Expectations

The first discovery enabler, seeing beyond your expectations, means noticing occurrences contrary to what you have preconceived. What is it that happens that defies your expectations? What are you overlooking and dismissing because you're looking only to see what you've seen before? If you take yourself off autopilot as an observer, you position yourself to break through your beliefs. That's when you begin to see new ways that might work better—sometimes new ways that are right in front of you—and which are most suitable for your particular situation.

The main way to ignite this form of seeing is by walking with others impacted by the situation to better understand their experience. "Walking with" is not an informal process, a casual get-together to "check things out." It is a purposeful exercise. This is just what DeltaCare clinicians and leaders engaged in when they walked the care path with patients. That's when they discovered new possibilities. Only when everyone got their eyes on the current reality—without projecting in its place an outdated reality—could they break through their prior beliefs.

To successfully implement an exercise of "walking with,"[2] however, you need first to deal with the main obstruction to seeing beyond your expectations. That obstruction is *selective attention*. This term refers to the finding in psychology that, in the midst of several other stimuli, humans can only process a limited set of them. When this happens, selective attention leads to inattentional blindness—the failure to notice an unexpected but fully visible occurrence. Seeing beyond what you expected to see then becomes difficult or impossible.

You may have seen the classic experiment featuring the "invisible" gorilla.[3] Participants who view a film of two teams passing basketballs are instructed to count the number of passes made by one of the teams. Halfway through, a woman wearing a gorilla suit appears, crosses the court, thumps her chest, and moves on. She is in view for nine seconds. It turns out that only about half of the participants mention the gorilla. Moreover, when the group that doesn't see the gorilla is told what the video actually showed, they insist the costumed woman never appeared.

The focus on one thing, counting, created inattentional blindness to another. That's one of the points of the experimenters, Daniel Simons and Christopher Chabris. Another lesson people typically take from the exercise is how little humans notice during an unfolding situation. The human brain plays attention tricks. But in the context of this book, you can see still another point, as shown by people's conviction that the gorilla never appeared: What you know to be true—your belief, your habits of expectations—can prevent you from discovering what you don't know. You excel at seeing what you expect to see, never mind the rest.

That's why this enabler is so critical. The experiment established people's expectation that they would see and be able to count the number of passes. Having accepted this expectation, most people simply didn't search for what they didn't know. They couldn't get beyond their expectations. Their belief, made rigid even in such a trivial experiment, suppressed the opportunity for discovery.

The power of expectation setting as an obstruction to this enabler is reinforced in more recent experiments by Trafton Drew, Melissa Võ, and Jeremy Wolfe. They again engaged the services of a gorilla, except that their experiment had a couple of twists.[4] Whereas early gorilla experiments involved naïve participants focused on unfamiliar tasks, Drew and his team asked expert participants, in this case doctors, to perform familiar tasks. Would the doctors, practicing their daily trade, be better at discovering what they didn't expect to see?

In the main experiment of three related studies, 24 radiologists were asked to search for nodules in five chest CT scans (computerized tomography) to detect lung cancer. Unknown to the doctors, the researchers had inserted into the fifth scan the image of a white-outlined gorilla that was 48 times the size of the average nodule.

Upon completing the five trials, participants were each asked what they saw. The questions were at first indirect. For example, "Did you notice anything unusual on the final trial?" At the end of questioning, they were asked directly: "Did you see a gorilla on the final trial?"

Twenty of the twenty-four, or 83 percent, of radiologist participants failed to report seeing the gorilla. Yet, by tracking the radiologists' eyes during their search of CT scans, researchers discovered that most of those doctors who didn't see the gorilla nevertheless had looked directly at its location. Drew, Võ, and Wolfe concluded that even experts working on familiar tasks in their professional area of expertise are susceptible to inattentional blindness. Expert or not, familiar with the task or not, people fail to see gorillas they're not looking for.

With too much confidence in knowing what to look at, you minimize your doubt. You fail to take account of what you might be missing. That encourages you to overlook the unknown and the unexpected that is in plain sight. The result? Even if you're an analytically minded physician, you suppress discovery of everything from silly gorillas to—in the case of BRI in chapter 1—the causes of surgical failures.

But when you see with the intention to break through your beliefs, you overcome years of selective attention—years of shutting out the overwhelming phenomena and stimuli that seek your attention. The French novelist Marguerite Duras wrote, "The art of seeing has to be learned." And that learning calls for engaging in a "walking with" exercise. You need an explicit means to force yourself to see that the new reality clashes with the former reality you have long believed in.

By engaging in a deliberate exercise of "walking with" others in a particular context, you learn how to become unshackled from inattentional blindness. That drives you to discover and adopt a new set of expectations beyond those you've long held. You turn seeing into an active process—not a passive one in which you distantly watch.

You do what O'Connell did. Rather than reading about homelessness, he walked straight into the apprenticeship with the nurses by caring for people in soaking their feet. With the help of McInnis, he expanded his ways of seeing. He discovered that, counter to his expectations developed during medical training, waiting for vulnerable groups of people to open up was more effective as health care than just starting out by giving medical advice.[5]

"Walking with" means that you go to see people in their natural context, rather than having them come to you—just as O'Connell did at Pine Street Inn, just as DeltaCare clinicians did who went into the units, just as the Intuit managers did who went into the small businesses. And just as did a lean consultant, an organizational ethnographer, a design consultant, or anyone who goes into human systems to better understand. All hope to discover what they don't know from close-up contact with the people who make up that system.

DeltaCare clinicians and leaders used the "walking with" exercise to find out whether their difficulties in mapping care flows were in fact, reality. To prepare for the activity, as described in chapter 2, they left their clinical garb and stethoscopes behind. Their goal was to see actual care through the patients' experience. By walking the flows with patients, the clinicians and leaders discovered that their beliefs about how care was delivered didn't match their observations. Not only were their mapping difficulties real, but their eyes could see how their system caused patients to struggle.

"Walking with" conveys a sense of getting closer to people's lived experience. As writer Anne Lamott says, "To be engrossed in something outside ourselves is a powerful antidote for the rational mind."[6] Lamott is right. Getting engrossed helps you see more clear-sightedly by paying attention in ways that overcome selective inattention. You pay close attention to what you are seeing—the details, clues, puzzles, struggles, and tensions in the context that can challenge what you expected to see. By paying attention in your seeing to your inattention, you may discover something that may have been long staring you in face but had until now remained hidden.

Permitting Recombination

Ironically, the same factors that make organizations successful all too readily produce their failure. Organizational theorist Danny Miller coined the term "Icarus Paradox"[7] to explain the phenomenon that businesses often fail subsequent to success. Overconfident leaders—having too little doubt—ignore a significant unintended consequence of success: belief rigidity. Simply put, everyone holds to the belief that all is going well. Unfortunately, as we saw in chapter 1, this belief quashes discovery of clues to the contrary.

In a 2018 interview,[8] Satya Nadella pointed to this rigidity as making it difficult to "reconflate [recombine] some of the capabilities across . . . divisions to build new products." He highlighted the associated challenge:

> We want to be able to take [these capabilities] and apply them to different markets at different times. Without this strategic flexibility, it's very, very hard. You need to be able to bring things

together. This is probably one of the more transformative changes that many CEOs will have to confront.

Nadella put into words what the second discovery enabler, permitting recombination, is all about. As a leader, you need to give license to others to recombine existing elements—such as capabilities, culture, people, processes, experiences, skills—in order to adjust to challenging situations and generate suitable, novel solutions. For example, Canlis leaders permitted staff to recombine elements as they redesigned operations for the initial three new pop-up businesses.

Recombination involves the activity of disconnecting and reconnecting to create a new combination of the existing elements. To begin with, it requires seeing with the intention to single out the reusable elements that are already present. Then you take up those elements separately and in relation, reflecting on them to get to know them and their value differently. What you are searching for is a satisfying "synthesis [among the elements] where everything will come together . . . like a jigsaw puzzle"[9] to resolve the challenging situation. For example, to address the negative experience of children with his MRI machine, Doug Dietz and his team recombined the elements of the lone big machine in the gray hospital room with the color, shapes, and materials of play. The hulking technology recombined well with the chairs and blankets Dietz saw children lovingly put to use in building forts and castles.

Generating new combinations of existing elements depends on your capacity to see new relationships between different elements, like Dietz and the Canlis leaders and staff did. But as a leader, it also requires that you give your leadership team and employees the green light to do recombination and that you equip them with two key resources to do it well: a broad and diversified menu of elements and exposure to different experiences.

Early on, for example, Nadella expanded elements for recombination when he told all Microsoft teams to share their software codes with one another. No longer did teams own codes. Any team could see another team's project and use that code. Nadella described this change as going "open source internally,"[10] quite a different practice from protecting one's knowledge, a hallmark of the former know-it-all culture.

As a leader, you also help build the capacity for recombination by permitting your leadership team and employees to gain exposure to diverse, new experiences and reflecting on them. In a 1996 interview,[11]

Steve Jobs provided insight into the important role of expansive experience in developing the capacity of recombination:

> When you ask . . . people how they did something . . . they didn't really *do* it, they just *saw* something [italics in original]. That's because they were able to connect experiences . . . and synthesize new things they were able to do that [because] they've had more experiences, or they have thought more about their experiences. A lot of people in our industry don't have enough dots to connect, and they end up with very linear solutions without a broad perspective on the problem. The broader one's understanding of the human experience, the better design [recombination] we will have.

Building out sets of elements and expanding human experience enables everyone to assemble a strong menu for recombination. The insight and new understandings that recombination produces help to creatively resolve the challenging situation.

Assessing Suitability of New Ways

The third enabler, assessing the suitability of proposed new ways, is based in the community's close-to-the-ground observation and experience with the situation. The work of assessing is iterative and fueled with the flexibility of belief—an openness by everyone even here to sustain the discovery process.

The assessment starts with deliberating and feeling out the fit and plausibility of the proposed new way. It continues through implementation of in-situ experiments with relevant stakeholder reflection. Depending on the insight and new understanding gained from the experiments, the new ways could be refined. Or additional in-situ experiments may be conducted. The work of assessing the new ways ends with community deliberation on the decision of whether or not, and if so, how to launch. The proposed new ways remain provisional until the community completes its assessment of the effectiveness of the chosen new ways to advance efforts in creating a new, satisfactory situation.

O'Connell and his colleagues sought to assess the suitability of a proposed new way of serving people experiencing homelessness. The winter of 1985 in Boston was especially cruel, causing a number of people to die on the streets without receiving care. O'Connell and others caring for the homeless persons in the shelters and soup kitchen learned that many of the deaths were among individuals who chronically slept outside rather than inside the shelters.

In response to these deaths, the Massachusetts Department of Health allocated Pine Street Inn the funds to operate an overnight van. "We knew we needed to get out to the streets," O'Connell said.[12] That was the start to deliberating and feeling out the plausibility of the proposed new way.

O'Connell participated in meetings at Pine Street Inn to develop the van. Despite his hopes that it would be a medical van, he found that the homeless persons participating in the meeting wanted the van to be a consistent presence. A van that would visit the streets nightly from 9 pm through 5 am and bring hot food, clothing, and warm blankets to distribute. While medical care could be offered, it would be secondary to the main mission of the van.

O'Connell was invited and spent two nights per week on the van. He served food and got to know people, offering medical care when possible. During the first two years of Covid, space on the van was limited, and he couldn't join at night but did continue daily street rounds. With vaccinations, O'Connell rejoined the van, splitting the two nights with Dave Munson (MD).

The in-situ experiment showed that operating the van *not* as a medical van was more conducive to serving people. O'Connell commented later that the recommendation to not create a medical van was "a brilliant way to get to know people on the streets who are pretty crusty ... scarred by not good encounters with the system."[13] For only after gaining trust would some people become open to medical treatment. That's when assessing the fit of a proposed new solution in its particular environs paid off.

Deciding to launch the proposed new solution of the van involved deliberation, as well as feeling out its potential viability and fit. Is this the way to proceed? Or not? Is medical treatment the focus for the van? Or not? Assessing whether and how to launch the new solution was a community decision based on what would best serve the purpose of meeting people on the streets. Launching the van provided further confidence that the proposed new way was helping to alleviate the troubling deaths that had occurred.

This is how assessing the suitability of new ways works to create successful launches. Always in context and with in-situ deliberation, experimentation, potential insight and reflection, and possible refinement. Once the relevant stakeholders complete their assessment of suitability, the chosen new ways are launched with the expectation that they will progress efforts in creating a new, satisfactory situation.

In the case of Pine Street Inn, since the van's implementation in 1986, it has never missed a night to support and provide care to people staying on the streets, averaging more than 80 visits per night.[14] O'Connell, in a van, had come through a full cycle of discovery to determine the van would work better than any other solutions.

SUMMARY

These stories of organizations using the third motor of discovery, launching new ways, showcase the power of situated action to creatively resolve situations that seem in the moment completely unworkable. When you are in situ, you are face-to-face with challenges and your struggles and tensions in dealing with them. This on-the-ground viewpoint is a markedly different situation than discussing those same challenges in a conference room away from the scene of action.

Canlis leaders and staff didn't need just imagination in developing the pop-up businesses. They needed improvisation to recombine roles and cooking responsibilities. O'Connell didn't need to privilege his medical knowledge in caring for people. He needed compassion and patience—and to hear the wisdom of the nurses. DeltaCare clinicians and leaders didn't need just knowledge of care flows. They needed to genuinely listen and have empathy for their patients' experiences. When you are in situ with others, you're in a no-turning-back moment that is a totally different lived experience from writing reports in an office or problem solving in the abstract.

In completing all three motors—capitalizing on surprise, harnessing genuine doubt, and launching new ways—you bring the full discovery cycle to a close. You see its unique power in a way you never did before. You initiated discovery when you realized that current beliefs failed to deal with new realities. Throughout it, you generated *ahas* and insights that helped you gain a clearer understanding of surprising facts that make better sense of the new reality. These discoveries prompted shifts in how you saw the world and opened new possibilities for action to make it work better. As you loosened your hold on prior beliefs and practice, you generated new ways to creatively address the unsettled situation. In the process, you recast the story of the unsettled situation, carving out an actionable path to transform the organization that you have confidence in. You have a story of purposeful action and success, not inertia and mediocrity.

The next two chapters show how the three motors and the discovery process can become a perpetual effort. These chapters show the importance of a relational infrastructure that undergirds discovery for human development and positive change. Building Capacity for Discovery (chapter 6) shows how central discovery-oriented connections and roles are to accomplishing dramatic behavioral change. Amplifying Discovery (chapter 7) demonstrates the benefits of going through multiple cycles of discovery, over time, with colleagues, building one on the other, to create and recreate organizations fit for the future.

~~~~~

1. The opportunity to see beyond our expectations often occurs when our beliefs are challenged. How can you use such a situation to develop your capacity to see with an intention to break through your beliefs?
2. Describe a time when you or others in your organization recombined existing elements to creatively resolve a challenging or puzzling situation. What was the result? How could you build on this experience?
3. How do you assess the suitability of proposed and promising new ways? Do you situate your efforts in the context of proposed implementation? How do you participate, listen, see, and feel in situ?

NOTES

1 The first section of this chapter (up to Launching New Ways) draws on the following sources. Moran, Barbara. 2016. "Street Doctor: How MED's Jim O'Connell Learned to Shelve His Stethoscope and Listen."

Bostonia. Winter/Spring. www.bu.edu/bostonia/winter-spring16/jim-oconnell-boston-health-care-for-the-homeless-program/, accessed June 2023; Neisloss, Liz. 2023 (March). "Dr. Jim O'Connell on Nearly Four Decades of Helping Boston's Unhoused." *WGBH Greater Boston News*. Video. www.youtube.com/watch?v=6amdiXRxEok, accessed June 2023; O'Connell, James J. 2015. *Stories from the Shadows: Reflections of a Street Doctor*. USA: The Boston Health Care for the Homeless Program Press; O'Connell, James J. 2004. "Dedication to Barbara M. McInnis." In *The HealthCare of Homeless Persons: A Manual of Communicable Diseases and Common Problems in Shelters & on the Streets*. Edited James J. O'Connell. Boston, MA: The Boston Health Care for the Homeless Program Press, pp. XIII–XIV; and Ruder, Debra Bradley. 2016. "Street Doctor: For Three Decades, James O'Connell Has Cared for the Homeless." *Harvard Magazine*. www.harvardmagazine.com/2016/01/street-doctor, accessed June 2023.

2 For further reading on this enabler, see Horowitz, Alexandra. 2013. *On Looking: A Walker's Guide to the Art of Observation*. New York: Scribner.

3 Simons, Daniel J., & Christopher F. Chabris. 1999. "Gorillas in Our Midst: Sustained Inattentional Blindness for Dynamic Events." *Perception* 28:1059–1074.

4 Drew, Trafton, Melissa L.H. Võ, & Jeremy M. Wolfe. 2013. "The Invisible Gorilla Strikes Again: Sustained Inattentional Blindness in Expert Observers." *Psychological Science* 24(9):1848–1853.

5 People who are unhoused have the highest mortality rate of any population subgroup in the US.

6 Lamott, Anne. 1995. *Bird by Bird: Some Instructions on Writing and Life*. New York: Anchor Books, p. 102.

7 Miller, Danny. 1992. *The Icarus Paradox: How Exceptional Companies Bring About Their Own Downfall*. New York: HarperCollins.

8 London, Simon. 2018. "Microsoft's Next Act: CEO Satya Nadella Talks About Innovation, Disruption and Organizational Change." *McKinsey Quarterly*. www.mckinsey.com/industries/technology-media-and-telecommunications/our-insights/ microsofts-next-act, accessed June 2023.

9 Young, James Webb. 2003. *A Technique for Producing Ideas*. USA: McGraw-Hill, p. 30.

10 Bort, Julie. 2014 (July 15). "Satya Nadella: This Is How I Am Really Going to Change Microsoft's Culture." *Business Insider*. https://finance.yahoo.com/news/satya-nadella-im-really-going-114355241.html

11 Wolf, Gary. 1996 (February 1). "Steve Jobs: The Next Insanely Great Thing." *Wired*. www.wired.com/1996/02/jobs-2/, accessed June 2023.

12 Cohan, Alexi. 2023 (March 2). "This Boston Doctor Has Cared for the Homeless for 40 Years. Here's What He Has Learned." *WGBH*. www.wgbh.org/news/local-news/2023/03/02/this-boston-doctor-has-cared-for-the-homeless-for-40-years-heres-what-hes-learned, accessed June 2023.

13 Neisloss, Liz. 2023 (March). "Dr. Jim O'Connell on Nearly Four Decades of Helping Boston's Unhoused." *WGBH Greater Boston News*. Video. www.youtube.com/ watch?v=6amdiXRxEok, accessed June 2023.
14 The website of Pine Street Inn: www.pinestreetinn.org/, accessed June 2023.

REFERENCES

Bort, Julie. 2014 (July 15). "Satya Nadella: This Is How I Am Really Going to Change Microsoft's Culture." *Business Insider*. https://finance.yahoo.com/news/satya-nadella-im-really-going-114355241.html

Cohan, Alexi. 2023 (March 2). "This Boston Doctor Has Cared for the Homeless for 40 Years. Here's What He Has Learned." *WGBH*. www.wgbh.org/news/local-news/2023/03/02/this-boston-doctor-has-cared-for-the-homeless-for-40-years-heres-what-hes-learned, accessed June 2023.

Drew, Trafton, Melissa L.H. Võ, & Jeremy M. Wolfe. 2013. "The Invisible Gorilla Strikes Again: Sustained Inattentional Blindness in Expert Observers." *Psychological Science* 24(9):1848–1853.

Horowitz, Alexandra. 2013. *On Looking: A Walker's Guide to the Art of Observation*. New York: Scribner.

Lamott, Anne. 1995. *Bird by Bird: Some Instructions on Writing and Life*. New York: Anchor Books.

London, Simon. 2018. "Microsoft's Next Act: CEO Satya Nadella Talks About Innovation, Disruption and Organizational Change." *McKinsey Quarterly*. www.mckinsey.com/industries/technology-media-and-telecommunications/our-insights/microsofts-next-act, accessed June 2023.

Miller, Danny. 1992. *The Icarus Paradox: How Exceptional Companies Bring About Their Own Downfall*. New York: HarperCollins.

Moran, Barbara. 2016. "Street Doctor: How MED's Jim O'Connell Learned to Shelve His Stethoscope and Listen." *Bostonia*. Winter/Spring. www.bu.edu/bostonia/winter-spring16/ jim-oconnell-boston-health-care-for-the-homeless-program/, accessed June 2023.

Neisloss, Liz. 2023 (March). "Dr. Jim O'Connell on Nearly Four Decades of Helping Boston's Unhoused." *WGBH Greater Boston News*. Video. www.youtube.com/ watch?v=6amdiXRxEok, accessed June 2023.

O'Connell, James J. 2004. "Dedication to Barbara M. McInnis." In *The HealthCare of Homeless Persons: A Manual of Communicable Diseases and Common Problems in Shelters & on the Streets*. Edited James J. O'Connell. Boston, MA: The Boston Health Care for the Homeless Program Institute Press, pp. XIII–XIV.

O'Connell, James J. 2015. *Stories from the Shadows: Reflections of a Street Doctor*. USA: Boston Healthcare for the Homeless Program Press.

Ruder, Debra Bradley. 2016. "Street Doctor: For Three Decades, James O'Connell Has Cared for the Homeless." *Harvard Magazine*. www.harvardmagazine.com/2016/01/ street-doctor, accessed June 2023.

Simons, Daniel J., & Christopher F. Chabris. 1999. "Gorillas in Our Midst: Sustained Inattentional Blindness for Dynamic Events." *Perception* 28:1059–1074.

Wolf, Gary. 1996 (February 1). "Steve Jobs: The Next Insanely Great Thing." *Wired*. www.wired.com/1996/02/jobs-2/, accessed June 2023.

Young, James Webb. 2003. *A Technique for Producing Ideas*. USA: McGraw-Hill.

6 Building Capacity for Discovery

In 1986, an estimated 3.5 million people contracted dracunculiasis annually in 17 sub-Saharan countries in Africa, as well as in Pakistan and India.[1] The disease dominated many people's lives in areas that were poor and without access to safe water.[2] Dracunculiasis has been a scourge for centuries, known by its common name, Guinea worm disease. Archeologists even point to Egyptian mummies with the worm's traces as evidence of its prevalence.[3]

The disease is caused by a parasite ingested in water contaminated by tiny crustaceans that carry Guinea worm larvae. The infection incubates without symptoms for 10 to 14 months, at which point the parasites break the skin in a lesion, most often on the lower limbs. It ends when the mature worm, which can grow up to three feet in length, erupts from the skin, typically from the foot, creating painful, burning sores.[4]

To extract the worm, people wind it on a small stick as it emerges. The stick gives them traction to pull the string-like worm from the wound a few centimeters daily, depending on their pain tolerance. Trained caregivers do the same, but also wind the worm on a small roll of sterile gauze.[5] Either way, people in pain naturally want to douse their burning limbs in water. But this contaminates the water source with new larvae.

International efforts to eradicate Guinea worm disease (GWD) began in 1980, as the world awoke to how the disease debilitated people for months. Afflicted people suffered from so much pain that they could not continue their schooling or farming. Nor could they supply food for their families. The eradication effort came on the heels of the successful campaign to eradicate smallpox, as the United

DOI: 10.4324/9781003513681-7

Nations (UN) declared the 1980s as the International Drinking Water Supply and Sanitation Decade (IDWSSD).

The UN's aim in its declaration was to provide safe drinking water and sanitation to all communities worldwide. At the US Centers for Disease Control and Prevention (CDC), Director William Foege (MD, MPH) and Donald Hopkins (MD, MPH) encouraged the IDWSSD steering committee to include dracunculiasis eradication in its efforts.[6] Since dracunculiasis is transmitted only by unsafe drinking water, the UN's efforts would *de facto* lead to eradication. In 1981, the committee adopted their request and supported GWD eradication as one of its goals.[7]

The story of eradicating GWD shows just how critical discovery-oriented connections and roles are for building the capacity to accomplish transformation in any organization. It highlights key features of these connections and roles, along with the enablers for success. The story also shows how leaders anywhere have to dedicate themselves to developing those connections and roles purposefully.

The Guinea worm campaign was especially ambitious as a project. If the campaign were to succeed, it would banish only the second disease from the earth. This would be a feat even greater than that of the smallpox eradication effort because the leaders of the partnerships could not turn to just a technological solution—a vaccine—to prevent the disease. Nor could they turn to medications to treat or cure the disease. They also could not count on infections to confer immunity to subsequent infections by the same person.

Their only alternative was to prevent human infection by educating residents on the origin and prevention and "empowering them to take action." The goal was to "change behavior enough to permanently interrupt transmission."[8] Villagers for the first time would have to filter their water. Sick people would have to stop dunking their burning limbs in public drinking supplies. The effort would require not just a solution from the outside. People on the inside would have to change their beliefs and behaviors.

Since 1986, the global campaign has been led by the Carter Center,[9] spearheaded by Hopkins and former President Jimmy Carter. In addition to global organizations such as the CDC, the World Health Organization, and the United Nations Children's Fund, leaders of the work ranged from health ministers to tribal chiefs, and thousands of village volunteers, as well as supervisory health staff, scientists, and public health experts. The transformation required called for involvement of people on multiple levels.

There were skeptics. Getting people to radically change behaviors and beliefs long practiced in the face of the disease was a tall order. Said Hopkins:

> People often said to us at the beginning . . . "This is not smallpox; you don't have a vaccine. You're going to have to change people's behavior—and you won't be able to do that." Well, lo and behold, it turns out if we approach people the right way and give them the information that they need, people will change their behavior—because they don't want to have Guinea worm, either. We don't have a vaccine to offer them, but we have something else: knowledge.[10]

The transformation began when the Carter Center and the CDC convened a multiday, multi-stakeholder meeting in Atlanta.[11] The group included 17 consultants, practitioners, and public health specialists—in particular, those from affected countries—to develop guidance for health education and community mobilization to prevent GWD in the endemic villages and areas.

Their work in Atlanta culminated in a set of guidelines[12] that shaped an education-driven eradication program. Hopkins and his colleague at the CDC, Ernesto Ruiz-Tiben (PhD), outlined a three-phase eradication strategy.[13] Phase 1 was to conduct baseline national surveys in affected countries. Phase 2 was to implement interventions through village-based workers who educate local populations on the Guinea worm life cycle and track disease-elimination progress. As cases declined, Phase 3 was to contain infected individuals in voluntary treatment centers to avoid further transmission.

Strikingly, since 1986, the number of reported cases of GWD has plunged by more than 99 percent. By 2007, case numbers had fallen to fewer than 10,000, and by 2012, to 542. In 2019, there were only 54 cases. And in 2022, the most recent reporting year, just 13 human cases were reported worldwide. The incidence of disease is so low that it hardly exists. Estimates suggest that more than 80 million cases have been prevented through the program's efforts. Experts consider the disease near eradication.[14] The case serves as a stellar example of not just how leaders can build the capacity for discovery, but also how the many organizations and many people served by those organizations can build the joint capacity to drive unprecedented results through the cycle of discovery.

THE RELATIONAL NATURE OF DISCOVERY

You can see how, at the personal level, you could think of discovery as a solo experience. Faced by an unsettled situation at work or in personal life, you could go through phases of a discovery cycle as part of a personal change in beliefs. You would experience a personal transformation furthering your success, but the impact wouldn't reach beyond yourself. Nor would the capacity to engage discovery expand in your hands to empower others. It could not transform your organization or community.

To have a substantive impact, you need people willing to join in the discovery process—people willing to grapple with the unsettled situation whose exploration and resolution matter. For the Carter Center, those people included stakeholders spread across the globe. They would tackle a situation that was centuries-old: the persistence of Guinea worm disease, the "forgotten disease of forgotten people."[15] This reflects a global effort aiming at a challenge similar to that of DeltaCare in chapter 2, as people across the organization tackled patients' troublesome struggles with the organization's delivery system. And it reflects the challenge similar to that of Microsoft, as everyone across the organization tackled the culture with a fixed mindset that hindered the company's growth and innovation.

Hopkins credits much of the success in eradicating GWD to the partnership's emphasis on the education efforts in the local communities.[16] That's what assured that the education in phase 2 brought about permanent changes in human behavior. Of course, many factors were critical in vanquishing the disease, but from the beginning, a critical one was that villagers were included in the campaign's efforts.

Marshall Kreuter (PhD, MPH), CDC behavioral health science educator at the time, described this approach. The leaders of institutions contributing to the global effort helped guide initial discovery. But he says,

> It is their [the villagers'] plan. Villagers themselves do this. They talk with one another . . . we get ideas from them. For example, the people trained in Atlanta went back and worked with villagers and local leaders, asking them, "How might we do this?"[17]

The cycle of discovery looped everyone into belief and behavior change.

DISCOVERY ENABLERS: BUILDING CAPACITY

When leaders assemble people to better understand challenging situations, they ignite possible connections across all sorts of boundaries, including geographic, demographic, expertise, and organizational. Each connection holds the potential to unlock insights and *ahas* that open new vantage points and never-before-considered possibilities. And over time, these connections build the capacity of many more people who can engage and conduct the process of discovery.

How do you build people's capacity to conduct and engage in discovery? Research points to the importance of three enablers: building diverse representation, fostering respectful engagement, and enacting flexible roles. Each enabler generates belief flexibility and meaningful involvement. You can put each to use at any point during the discovery cycle to build and benefit from everyone's know-how and experience. Without these enablers, you risk derailing the discovery process.

Building Diverse Representation

The first enabler, build diverse representation, directs leaders to grow a diversity of connections, in particular those of relevance to exploring the unsettled situation or new reality. In one respect, this enabler highlights the obvious: leaders need to consider more than a narrow bandwidth of people. They assemble members with different practices, roles, perspectives, skills, ideas, tools, and experience.

But, as shown in the last chapter, such diversity—especially diverse experience—lays the foundation for recombining old elements in new ways. Recombination generates insights, which people can use to create novel solutions to unsettled situations or new realities. Diversity also enriches the reservoir of possible ideas and meanings for use in understanding these situations.

Leaders also need to factor in members' diverse connections to the particular context. For example, specific to the eradication program, former President Jimmy Carter stayed in contact with national leaders of countries affected by the disease. He did this through personal communications and annual trips to Africa to meet with national leaders. During those visits, he met with presidents and health ministers and asked for their support and encouraged them to visit their affected communities. He also invited former leaders to become ambassadors and advocates for GWD eradication with their people.

Through his efforts, President Carter excelled in garnering critical political will for the national dracunculiasis eradication program.[18]

Looking from a distance at the Guinea worm eradication program, it is easy to see the diversity of partners' geography and expertise. When looking closer at the specific context of the effort to eradicate the centuries-old debilitating disease, you see even more diversity. Embraced in this global effort are people and organizations at every level, including villagers whose way of living depended on the success of the effort.

At DeltaCare, Kathryn Correia similarly cast a wide net for diverse stakeholders with the dedication to dig into the future viability of their health delivery system. She not only invited the expected people to join—clinicians and administrators—but also people including patients, volunteers, and board members. She included people who directly affected care and could contribute as well as others who were impacted by how that care was delivered.

Canlis leaders (chapter 4) also included not just their senior people but all interested staff. They asked everyone to become involved in launching the new pop-up businesses. Looking from a distance, you see the diversity in hierarchical level and type of role. However, when looking closer at the specific context of other restaurant closures and significant job losses during a pandemic, you see more than structural diversity. Embraced in this effort were people whose livelihoods depended on this restaurant's success.

As the stories of Guinea worm eradication, DeltaCare, and Canlis show, building a diverse representation of people who impact, or who are impacted by, the focal concern is critical to growing quality connections that build the capacity of discovery.

Building diverse representation is not a one-time event. It requires continual effort as issues, people, and contexts change. In eradicating GWD, for example, Carter, Hopkins, and Ruiz-Tiben continued to grow connections even after they had made extensive global ones early on. Their efforts have resulted in the campaign reaching more than 23,000[19] local villages with support to assure the ongoing education needed to achieve eradication. As one study[20] reported, "the primacy of intensive community effort" was a key factor in the initiative's success.[21]

Fostering Respectful Engagement

Simply meeting a diverse set of people around a table to discuss an unsettled situation doesn't yield discovery. This assembly needs to do more than "allow" people to have input. Leaders need to actively engage with people's differences in a way that conveys genuine mutual interest. People need to know that their input is valued and that it could alter the course of action.[22] That requires leaders to focus their attention on the practices of respectful engagement.

Four studies[23] by Jane Dutton of University of Michigan's Ross School of Business, Ashley Hardin of Washington University's Olin Business School, and Abraham Carmeli of Tel Aviv University's Coller School of Management show how this second enabler supports discovery. They characterize respectful engagement as working with others in a way that "conveys a sense of presence, worth, and positive regard." One key finding for discovery is that engaging respectfully encourages reflection on unique ideas and different combinations of perspectives.

During his earlier work to eradicate smallpox, Hopkins' approach embodied this kind of engagement. He had seen too many interactions with villagers that were the opposite of respectful engagement. He described what usually happened when international health workers entered villages and towns in Asia and Africa:

> They'd come with this attitude: "I have degrees. I am from America. And I am here to tell you what to do, you ignorant people." . . . [But] people, no matter how materially poor they are, no matter their circumstances, they pick up on that and they resent it.[24]

By contrast, Hopkins and others assured that the global efforts to eradicate GWD were driven by respect for the local villages and towns, coupled with education as the method of discovering knowledge about the disease. From Carter and Hopkins outward, engaging in respectful human connections was neither window dressing nor pro forma outreach. Field workers did not tell villagers what to do, nor did they just politely gather villagers' input and then leave. Rather, they listened empathically, a core practice of respectful engagement.

Empathic listening means being "tuned in enough to genuinely hear" other persons' perspectives and emotions.[25] It is more than giving someone else air space to talk, and it is more than simply acknowledging their presence. It is a choice you make in the moment to pay attention and feel concern for what others are going through. Hopkins shared:

> The most fundamental thing is putting yourself in the position of the people that you're trying to help—never disrespecting them and knowing that they may not trust you or other health workers

and may be unwilling to listen. Your job is to help them understand why it's in their interest to change their behavior. What's in it for them? It's not seeing numbers coming down on a chart or in a table, and it's not making people from another country feel better. It's that this is a terrible disease and, my God, we can stop it, we don't have to keep suffering from it.

Listening empathically fuels discovery of new perspectives. That's because it activates the motor of surprise. When you look for and are willing to be surprised by feeling what others are feeling, you connect more deeply with the concerns of others. This connection in turn can catalyze insight into puzzling situations. For example, we saw in chapter 2 how in connecting more deeply with their patients' struggles to get care, DeltaCare leaders and clinicians opened themselves to the full extent of surprise of fragmented care. Similarly, only when Intuit leaders (chapter 3) connected more closely with their customers to figure out puzzling survey results did they open themselves to the surprise. That is when they discovered that their customers actually used Quicken, a home product, for small business bookkeeping. That spurred an *aha* moment that led to a much larger market opportunity.

An openness to surprise during engagement was critical in eradicating GWD. Although scientific knowledge about how to prevent the disease existed, the leaders, field workers, and public health scientists did not presume to have all the answers. They knew it would take more than scientific knowledge for the initiative to succeed. They would listen in order to better understand how beliefs and practices affected the transmission of GWD.[26]

Through respectful engagement, field workers discovered two beliefs that affected transmission. First, some villagers believed that the Guinea worm was a normal part of their body, sometimes described as a protruding nerve,[27] and thus could not be avoided. Second, villagers believed that their local water was sacred.[28] It is the source of life. However, what many villagers didn't know was that that same sacred water was the origin of Guinea worm disease.

Rather than dismissing prevailing beliefs and imposing new ones onto the villagers, everyone from the field workers to Hopkins and Carter respected the traditional beliefs.[29] For example, described Hopkins:

> You don't directly challenge those beliefs because you're not going to win. Instead, try to sidestep the belief by saying, "Well, that

may be true, but here's what your neighbors did, and it helped them to get rid of this Guinea worm disease." Of course, it helps to have people whom they already respect conveying this information: traditional leaders, religious leaders, village chiefs, local teachers, local health workers, and testimonials from the people next door It's not that they continued suffering from Guinea worm because they wanted to they didn't understand how to not suffer from it.

Field workers combined the practice of empathic listening with sharing knowledge about GWD. They wanted every citizen in every village[30] to have the opportunity to understand the origin and life cycle of GWD. Together, field and village health workers would start by meeting with villagers at their local water source. They would ask: Can you tell me what you know about Guinea worm disease?[31] That question and follow-on discussion kicked off a process in which the people discovered the life cycle and origins of the disease. The cycle that informed their discovery process is developed in Figure 6.1.

Along with discussion, health workers gave a visual demonstration. Filling a bucket with unfiltered pond water, they filtered it and poured the backwash into a jar. The villagers could then see in the concentrated liquid tiny aquatic fleas—the same fleas that carry Guinea worm larvae.[32] Surprised at seeing the worms, villagers would invariably respond: There is something in the water!

The health workers would respond in turn, offering the jar for the villagers to drink. But upon examining the contaminants, the villagers refused. When people see "live things," said one health worker,

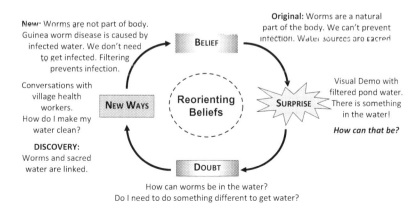

FIGURE 6.1 Generating new ways to treat a centuries-old disease.

they "get" Guinea worm and understand its connection to drinking water.[33] The health workers would then remind villagers that the contents of this jar are exactly what they drink if they choose not to filter their water.

The new reality of seeing worms in the water was, for many villagers, the first time they discovered the link between the sacred water and the nasty disease. It was also the first time many saw live worms separate from their body. The seeming contradictions challenged their beliefs and generated many questions that signaled doubts about what they had previously understood. How could these worms that caused the terrible disease be in the sacred water? Don't they live in everyone's body? Do I trust that this is the case? If so, how can I make the water clean?

The field and village health workers would follow with repeated demonstrations and education sessions, including knowledge about how to filter pond water. Each time, they answered villagers' questions—again respecting traditional beliefs while integrating an understanding of the new scientific information. The villagers' response was not unlike the response of many people going through the discovery process in wildly different situations. At first, there is incredulity, and then with support, they capitalize on their surprise for discovery. Then they experience genuine doubt, together, before deciding to try the new practice of filtering unfiltered water.

The contribution village health workers continue to make to this process is noteworthy. As villagers themselves, trained by international field workers in health education, they shared the knowledge and encouraged people to adopt the filtering practice, even though many believed the filters would not work as promised. The result? In villages without village health workers, without the local connection, "acceptance was quite low."[34]

In time and across thousands of villages, this approach helped villagers loosen their hold on prevailing beliefs. They could start to see that the worm was not a natural part of their body, and that it was not spirits resident in water sources that were punishing them. They could then change their practice of drinking unfiltered water.

Designing Flexibility Into Roles

Traditionally, people who guide initiatives such as new product design, cultural change, or innovation play established roles. Designers are differentiated from implementers. Teachers from students.

Experts from non-experts. Innovators from adopters. With responsibility and authority divided, their traditional roles help stabilize boundaries between them.

But this division weakens connections across boundaries and diminishes opportunities to grow them. People find it difficult to feel included.[35] For this reason, the third discovery enabler highlights the importance of designing flexible roles that support connections across boundaries.

Take the example of the expert role—consultant, leader, scientist. As leader of discovery, you will need to manage tensions that arise when experts assume a know-it-all stance. Operating from this stance, experts all too easily dominate conversation and dismiss others' input. As developed in chapter 4, these experts have too much confidence in their own knowledge. As a result, they lack the ability to engage what they don't know.

But that's where this enabler comes in. When you invite experts who are secure enough in their expertise to recognize the contribution of others without being all-knowing—to be confident *and* humble[36]—you grow connections that assure input from all and continuing opportunities for discovery. That's what happened in the Guinea worm eradication efforts.

Public health experts, for example, could easily have projected too much confidence in their knowledge as scientists and dismissed villager beliefs as inconsequential. But with confident humility, they gradually gained the trust of villagers and village chiefs. As CDC health science educator Kreuter explained:

> We don't leave the science stuff behind; we listen to villagers' input and adjust what we do. We may have plan A and B possibilities, but we are flexible. Often, we move to plan W or X if the situation is different than originally thought. This isn't less scientific, it is more responsive, and cultivates villager agency.[37]

In holding their knowledge as fallible, the scientists stayed open to discovering something they didn't know. They are there to help villagers whose lives were altogether different from theirs, after all. They still had confidence in what they know. But at the same time, they remained open and *flexible*, as Kreuter said, and prepared to *adjust* what they did in the face of unexpected input or new experience.

One of the groups afflicted with the Guinea worm was the Tuareg people, who provide an illuminating example of just how powerful flexible roles are in spurring discovery. The Tuareg's efforts to eradicate the disease took on a life of its own. Instead of only adopting practices others had created, the Tuareg took on the role of innovator. They spurred an explosion of discovery far away from the original leaders who lit the discovery fuse.

The Tuareg are a nomadic people who live in the Sahara Desert of Africa. They invented new and now-ubiquitous filter pipes. To create their invention, they attached small bits of water-filter cloth to the end of dried reeds. The filter-outfitted reeds then became straws they tied around their neck for on-the-go filtration.[38] That prompted a reverse flow of discovery. Industry partners then made a more durable version of the pipe filter to distribute to every at-risk individual in Sudan.[39]

Eventually, a Danish company, Vestergaard, commercialized the filter, LifeStraw.® Since 1999, the company has donated pipe and household cloth filters to villagers in need. To this day, the filter remains in use, preventing thousands of people from becoming infected with GWD.

The boundary between innovator and adopter also became flexible when villagers tailored education methods to the local context, making filtering more acceptable and easier to do on a daily basis. Some villagers wrote new songs in local languages that describe the Guinea worm's life cycle and what people need to do to break the cycle. Still others produced posters near water sources that show contrasting examples—one of a woman who filtered her water with no Guinea worm and one of a woman who did not filter her water and has a worm emerging from her body.

The boundary between traditional teacher and student roles became more flexible as well. In 2016, Hopkins noted the power of that flexibility. The global community had discovered, he said, the "potential power of health education" and "the power of village volunteers, particularly women, to effect real change in their communities."[40]

SUMMARY

The story of the program to eradicate Guinea worm disease illuminates the power of growing connections across different schools of knowledge to foster meaningful behavioral change. Scientific knowledge about the disease is critical to the education process and essential for eradication. But by itself, it is not sufficient to produce the dramatic level of behavioral change.

Success required respectful engagement that catalyzed *thousands* of one-to-one interactions that encouraged people to try the new practice of filtering unfiltered water. It took flexibility in the beliefs of field and health workers to implement education that enabled people to discover for themselves that the worm was not a natural part of their body. And it took flexibility of roles for everyone to create new ways to educate others and prevent the spread of Guinea worm disease. Discovery is relational in its core connections.

The next chapter shows how to amplify discovery for larger benefits. It continues the story of DeltaCare from chapter 2 to show how clinicians and leaders combine multiple cycles of discovery, each building one on the other. For DeltaCare, that was an imperative in creating a new model of delivering patient care.

~~~~~

1. Select one discovery enabler from this chapter: building diverse representation, fostering respectful engagement, designing flexibility into roles. Imagine using that enabler more consistently. What actions do you take? How do you feel when using it? What thoughts run through your mind?
2. Think of a time when your organization, team, or local community underwent a successful transformation process—where at least one belief changed. What discovery enablers did leaders and group members use to build the capacity of those involved to engage discovery?
3. A key part of fostering respectful engagement is listening empathically. Can you think of a time when you listened empathically? What did it feel like? Did you discover new perspectives? Did it lead to an insight or *aha* moments for you?

NOTES

1 Watts, Susan J. 1987. "Dracunculiasis in Africa in 1986: Its Geographic Extent, Incidence and at-Risk Population." *American Journal of Tropical Medicine and Hygiene* 37(1):119–125.
2 World Health Organization. 1991. *Guidelines for Health Education and Community Mobilization in Dracunculiasis Eradication Programs.* World Health Organization Collaborating Center for Research, Training and Eradication of Dracunculiasis. Centers for Disease Control and Prevention, p. 4 https://www.who.int/publications/i/item/guidelines-for-health-education-and-community-mobilization-in-dracunculiasise

radication-programs, accessed June 2023; Green, Lawrence W., Andrea Carlson Gielen, Judith M. Ottoson, Darleen V. Peterson, & Marshall W. Kreuter. 2022. *Health Program Planning, Implementation and Evaluation: Creating Behavioral, Environmental and Policy Change.* Baltimore: Johns Hopkins University Press, p. 5.

3. Carter Center. "Guinea Worm: Countdown to Zero Timeline." www.cartercenter.org/resources/gallery/images/highres/guineaworm_timeline.pdf, accessed June 2022; Basu, Moni. 2016 (May 6). "Donald Hopkins Helped Kill Smallpox and Is Close to Slaying the Fiery Serpent." *CNN Health.* www.cnn.com/2016/05/06/health/man-who-kills-disease/index.html, accessed June 2023; McNeil, Donald G. 2014 (October 23). "Inching Toward Eradication." *New York Times.* www.nytimes.com/2014/10/26/arts/artsspecial/jimmy-carters-fight-against-the-guinea-worm.html, accessed June 2023.

4. An illustration of the life cycle of *Dracunculus medinensis* is available on the Centers for Disease Control and Prevention website: www.cdc.gov/dpdx/dracunculiasis/ index.html.

5. Ruiz-Tiben, Dr. Ernesto. June 3, 2023. Email correspondence. In addition, the trained caregivers keep skin lesions free of infection via daily applications of topical antibiotics and bandages. During this process, patients are isolated at home or at a health facility and receive education about the origin of their infection and how to prevent a future infection. The average incapacity period from dracunculiasis is four to eight weeks. Case containment "shortens the period of incapacity to about a week, depending on how many worms may emerge, and prevents permanent disability."

6. Interview with Dr. Ernesto Ruiz-Tiben, PhD, Former Director (1998–2018) Dracunculiasis Eradication Program, The Carter Center.

7. Carter Center. "Guinea Worm: Countdown to Zero Timeline." www.cartercenter.org/resources/gallery/images/highres/guineaworm_timeline.pdf, accessed June 2022.

8. Ruiz-Tiben, Dr. Ernesto. June 3, 2023. Email correspondence.

9. Hopkins, Donald R., Ernesto Ruiz-Tiben, Mark L. Eberhard, Adam Weiss, P. Craig Withers, Jr., Sharon L. Roy, & Dean G. Sienko. 2018. "Dracunculiasis Eradication: Are We There Yet?" *The American Journal of Tropical Medicine and Hygiene* 99(2):388–395.

10. Drexler, Madeline. 2018. "Fierce Optimism." *Harvard Public Health.* Winter. www. hsph.harvard.edu/magazine/magazine_article/fierce-optimism/, accessed June 2023.

11. Dr. Donald Hopkins and his colleague, Dr. Ernesto Ruiz-Tiben, at the time leaders in the WHO Collaborating Center for Eradication of Dracunculiasis at CDC, received funding from the United Nations to develop guidelines for health education and community development across the endemic countries.

12. World Health Organization. 1991. *Guidelines for Health Education and Community Mobilization in Dracunculiasis Eradication Programs.* World Health Organization Collaborating Center for Research, Training and Eradication of Dracunculiasis. Centers for Disease Control and Prevention.

13. Hopkins, D.R., & Ernesto Ruiz-Tiben. 1991. "Strategies for Dracunculiasis Eradication." *Bulletin of the World Health Organization.*

14 Green, Lawrence W., Andrea Carlson Gielen, Judith M. Ottoson, Darleen V. Peterson, & Marshall W. Kreuter. 2022. *Health Program Planning, Implementation and Evaluation: Creating Behavioral, Environmental and Policy Change.* Baltimore: Johns Hopkins University Press, p. 5.
15 Ruiz-Tiben, Dr. Ernesto. June 6, 2023. Phone conversation. The phrase "Guinea worm warriors" was initially coined to describe the tremendous dedication of village health workers to eradication education and prevention practices. Over the years, this phrase came to represent all involved with the Guinea Worm Eradication program, regardless of their location or role in the effort.
16 World Health Organization. 1991. *Guidelines for Health Education and Community Mobilization in Dracunculiasis Eradication Programs.* World Health Organization Collaborating Center for Research, Training and Eradication of Dracunculiasis. Centers for Disease Control and Prevention, p. 27; Basu, Moni. 2016 (May 6). "Donald Hopkins Helped Kill Smallpox and Is Close to Slaying the Fiery Serpent." *CNN Health.* www.cnn.com/2016/05/06/health/man-who-kills-disease/index.html, accessed June 2023.
17 Interview with Dr. Marshall Kreuter (PhD, MPH), former CDC behavioral health science educator.
18 Ruiz-Tiben, Dr. Ernesto. June 3, 2023. Email correspondence.
19 Ghebreyesus, Dr. T.A., & Jason Carter. 2022. "This Is How We Finish Off Guinea Worm." https://www.globalcause.co.uk/malaria/malaria-and-ntds/this-is-how-we-finish-offguinea-worm/, accessed June 2023.
20 Awofeso, Niyi. 2013. "Towards Global Guinea Worm Eradication in 2015: The Experience of South Sudan." *International Journal of Infectious Diseases*: 17:e579.
21 Ibid.
22 Quick, Kathryn S., & Martha S. Feldman. 2011. "Distinguishing Participation and Inclusion." *Journal of Planning Education and Research* 31(3):272–290.
23 Carmeli, Abraham, Jane E. Dutton, & Ashley E. Hardin. 2015. "Respect as an Engine for New Ideas: Linking Respectful Engagement, Relational Information Processing and Creativity Among Employees and Teams." *Human Relations* 68(6):1021–1047.
24 Basu, Moni. 2016 (May 6). "Donald Hopkins Helped Kill Smallpox and Is Close to Slaying the Fiery Serpent." *CNN Health.* www.cnn.com/2016/05/06/health/man-who-kills-disease/index.html, accessed June 2023.
25 Worline, Monica C., & Jane E. Dutton. 2017. *Awakening Compassion at Work.* Oakland, CA: Berrett-Koehler Publishers.
26 Basu, Moni. 2016 (May 6). "Donald Hopkins Helped Kill Smallpox and Is Close to Slaying the Fiery Serpent." *CNN Health.* www.cnn.com/2016/05/06/health/man-who-kills-disease/index.html, accessed June 2023.
27 Awofeso, Niyi. 2013. "Towards Global Guinea Worm Eradication in 2015: The Experience of South Sudan." *International Journal of Infectious Diseases*: 17:e579.
28 Lazaro, Fred de Sam. 2010 (April 7). "Eradicating Guinea Worm, Step by Step." *Public Broadcasting NewsHour.* www.pbs.org/newshour/health/eradicating-guinea-worm-step-by-step, accessed June 2023.
29 Ibid.

30 World Health Organization. 1991. *Guidelines for Health Education and Community Mobilization in Dracunculiasis Eradication Programs.* World Health Organization Collaborating Center for Research, Training and Eradication of Dracunculiasis. Centers for Disease Control and Prevention.
31 Carter Center. Late 1980s. Guidelines for health education and community mobilization in dracunculiasis eradication programs. The idea of a visual demonstration in education is a public health tenet described in the guidelines document. It was creatively adapted for use.
32 Drexler, Madeline. 2018. "Fierce Optimism." *Harvard Public Health.* Winter. www. hsph.harvard.edu/magazine/magazine_article/fierce-optimism/, accessed June 2023.
33 Al Jazeera English. "Lifelines—How to Slay a Dragon." *YouTube.* Video. www.you-tube.com/watch?v=znRQvTCJvy0, accessed June 2023.
34 World Health Organization. 1991. *Guidelines for Health Education and Community Mobilization in Dracunculiasis Eradication Programs.* World Health Organization Collaborating Center for Research, Training and Eradication of Dracunculiasis. Centers for Disease Control and Prevention, p. 61. https://www.who.int/publications/i/ item/guidelines-for-health-education-and-community-mobilization-in-dracunculiasiseradication-programs, accessed June 2023.
35 Quick, Kathryn S., & Martha S. Feldman. 2011. "Distinguishing Participation and Inclusion." *Journal of Planning Education and Research* 31(3):272–290.
36 Grant, Adam. 2021. *Think Again: The Power of Knowing What You Don't Know.* New York: Viking. Developed in chapter 4.
37 Interview with Dr. Marshall Kreuter (PhD, MPH), former CDC behavioral health science educator.
38 VOA News. 2009 (November). "Simple Way to Prevent Guinea Worm Disease." www. voanews.com/a/a-13-2009-04-06-voa21–68731222/ 409863.html, accessed June 2023.
39 Carter Center. 2018 (March). "South Sudan Stops Transmission of Guinea Worm Disease." www.cartercenter.org/news/pr/guinea-worm-032118.html, accessed June 2023.
40 Carter Center. 2016 (April 4). "Q&A on the Historic Guinea Worm Eradication Campaign with Dr. Donald Hopkins and Dr. Ernesto Ruiz-Tiben." www.cartercenter.org/ news/documents/doc2224.html, accessed June 2023.

REFERENCES

Al Jazeera English. "Lifelines—How to Slay a Dragon." *YouTube.* Video. www.youtube. com/watch?v=znRQvTCJvy0, accessed June 2023.

Awofeso, Niyi. 2013. "Towards Global Guinea Worm Eradication in 2015: The Experience of South Sudan." *International Journal of Infectious Diseases* 17:e577–e582.

Basu, Moni. 2016 (May 6). "Donald Hopkins Helped Kill Smallpox and Is Close to Slaying the Fiery Serpent." *CNN Health.* www.cnn.com/2016/05/06/health/man-who-kills-disease/index.html, accessed June 2023.

Carmeli, Abraham, Jane E. Dutton, & Ashley E. Hardin. 2015. "Respect as an Engine for New Ideas: Linking Respectful Engagement, Relational Information Processing and Creativity Among Employees and Teams." *Human Relations* 68(6):1021–1047.

Carter Center. "Guinea Worm: Countdown to Zero Timeline." www.cartercenter.org/ resources/gallery/images/highres/guineaworm_timeline.pdf, accessed June 2022.

Carter Center. 2016 (April 4). "Q&A on the Historic Guinea Worm Eradication Campaign with Dr. Donald Hopkins and Dr. Ernesto Ruiz-Tiben." www.cartercenter.org/news/documents/doc2224.html, accessed June 2023.

Carter Center. 2018 (March). "South Sudan Stops Transmission of Guinea Worm Disease." www.cartercenter.org/news/pr/guinea-worm-032118.html, accessed June 2023.

Drexler, Madeline. 2018. "Fierce Optimism." *Harvard Public Health*. Winter. www. hsph.harvard.edu/magazine/magazine_article/fierce-optimism/, accessed June 2023.

Ghebreyesus, Dr. T.A., & Jason Carter. 2022. "This Is How We Finish Off Guinea Worm."https://www.globalcause.co.uk/malaria/malaria-and-ntds/this-is-how-we-finish-off-guinea-worm/, accessed June 2023.

Grant, Adam. 2021. *Think Again: The Power of Knowing What You Don't Know*. New York: Viking.

Green, Lawrence W., Andrea Carlson Gielen, Judith M. Ottoson, Darleen V. Peterson, & Marshall W. Kreuter. 2022. *Health Program Planning, Implementation and Evaluation: Creating Behavioral, Environmental and Policy Change*. Baltimore: Johns Hopkins University Press.

Hopkins, Donald R., & Ernesto Ruiz-Tiben. 1991. "Strategies for Dracunculiasis Eradication." *Bulletin of the World Health Organization* 69(5):533–540.

Hopkins, Donald R., Ernesto Ruiz-Tiben, Mark L. Eberhard, Adam Weiss, P. Craig Withers, Jr., Sharon L. Roy, & Dean G. Sienko. 2018. "Dracunculiasis Eradication: Are We There Yet?" *The American Journal of Tropical Medicine and Hygiene* 99(2):388–395. McNeil, Donald G. 2014 (October 23). "Inching Toward Eradication." *New York Times*. www.nytimes.com/2014/10/26/arts/artsspecial/jimmy-carters-fight against-the-guinea-worm.html, accessed June 2023.

Quick, Kathryn S., & Martha S. Feldman. 2011. "Distinguishing Participation and Inclusion." *Journal of Planning Education and Research* 31(3):272–290.

Ruiz-Tiben, Dr. Ernesto. June 3, 2023. Email correspondence.

Ruiz-Tiben, Dr. Ernesto. June 6, 2023. Phone conversation.

VOA News. 2009 (November). "Simple Way to Prevent Guinea Worm Disease." www. voanews.com/a/a-13-2009-04-06-voa21–68731222/409863.html, accessed June 2023.

Watts, Susan J. 1987. "Dracunculiasis in Africa in 1986: Its Geographic Extent, Incidence and at-Risk Population." *American Journal of Tropical Medicine and Hygiene* 37(1):119–125.

World Health Organization. 1991. *Guidelines for Health Education and Community Mobilization in Dracunculiasis Eradication Programs.* World Health Organization Collaborating Center for Research, Training and Eradication of Dracunculiasis. Centers for Disease Control and Prevention. https://www.who.int/publications/i/item/guidelines-for-health-education-and-community-mobilization-in-dracunculiasis-eradication-programs, accessed June 2023.

Worline, Monica C., & Jane E. Dutton. 2017. *Awakening Compassion at Work.* Oakland, CA: Berrett-Koehler Publishers.

Amplifying Discovery

You might be thinking by this point in the book that discovery can serve as a powerful one-time tool at any crossroads in organizational life. It yields a world of benefits, even if you tap it just to adjust one organizational belief. But like most tools, it has a multiplier effect when used repeatedly. It spawns consecutive insights and *ahas* that spur belief and behavior change for full transformation.

That was the experience of the leaders at DeltaCare,[1] who led the organization through five cycles of discovery. Their commitment to conducting multiple cycles enabled them to create an innovative new model of care that markedly improved patient and staff outcomes. Only after going through all cycles could everyone move away from old beliefs and toward new ones that supported their truly patient-centered care model. Only then could they evolve their purpose and reorient their beliefs to both kick off the change and drive it to completion.

Table 7.1 shows the full set of discovery cycles conducted by the participants[2] profiled in this chapter.

DeltaCare's Kathryn Correia and her stakeholders—DeltaCare leaders, clinicians, patients, and other stakeholders—could have quit after one round of discovery. In surfacing their inability to map care flows in the first round, and in walking those care flows, they brought operational weaknesses into focus. That's where we left the story in chapter 2. All stakeholder participants could then easily see that they hurt patient care by practicing "heroics," by allowing "fragmentation," and by leaving in their wake "frustrated patients."

The first cycle had the intended, beneficial effect. Caregivers and administrators recognized they had to embrace a new belief: The

DOI: 10.4324/9781003513681-8

118 AMPLIFYING DISCOVERY

TABLE 7.1 Full Set of Discovery Cycles: Creating New Ways of Delivering Patient Care

	C1: Engage the unexpected situation	C2: Deepen understanding of unexpected situation	C3: Generate future objects	C4: Elaborate new ways	C5: Negotiate new ways
Current Belief	Mapping care flows is straightforward.	Care is fragmented. Mapping obstacles is straightforward.	Patient data is collected effectively. Independent clinicians deliver optimal care.	Clinicians work independently. Working as a team won't be easy.	Tollgates erode clinician, especially physician, authority and independence.
Catalyze surprise	Mapping care flows is more difficult than expected. What does this mean?	Mapping obstacles is more difficult than expected. Something isn't right.	Negative patient input about clinicians not working well together. Why not talk to each other?	Nursing used negative patient input to propose trio. Will it work?	Direct challenge by physicians. "I really don't like this."
Harness genuine doubt	Could the difficulty in mapping care flows stem from real difficulties in care?	How do we not know how patients get out of our system?	Clinicians: Could we be responsible for causing confusion in care?	Clinician hesitancy and discomfort. How will we ask questions in front of the patient?	We're at an impasse. Tollgates not working. Conflict among clinicians.

(Continued)

AMPLIFYING DISCOVERY   119

TABLE 7.1 (Continued)

	C1: Engage the unexpected situation	C2: Deepen understanding of unexpected situation	C3: Generate future objects	C4: Elaborate new ways	C5: Negotiate new ways
Search for resolution to doubt	Walking actual care flows.	Map flows instead of continuing to map obstacles.	What would it look like if clinicians talked with each other? Patient 'collaborative' idea resonated.	6-week offsite practice session.	Three events with clinicians to resolve conflict. New data in 3rd.
Discovery	*Flow is fragmented. We are deeply disturbed.*	*System itself is the problem. Need to redesign care.*	*'Collaborative' signifies future.*	*It works!*	*Breakthrough agreement in 3rd event.*
New Belief	Mapping care flows is difficult. Real obstacles cause patient hardship. Must minimize them.	Need 'whole new paradigm' to become "truly-patient centered."	Data wasn't collected effectively. Clinicians collaborate with each other and patient at the bedside.	Clinicians deliver optimal care as an interdisciplinary team at the patient bedside.	Revised Tollgate clarified expectations that deliver optimal care.
Evolution	Establish purpose	Evolve purpose	'Collaborative care' future object	Gain assurance of 'Trio' as element in new ways	Regain assurance of 'Tollgate' as element in new ways

120 AMPLIFYING DISCOVERY

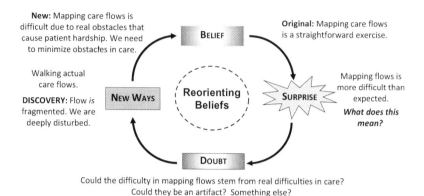

FIGURE 7.1 Engage the unexpected situation.

only way to put their house in order was to minimize obstacles to integrated care. Up until then, they had held faulty beliefs that their behaviors *did* focus on patients and *did* provide integrated care flows. The new beliefs allowed all of them, the clinicians in particular—doctors, nurses, and pharmacists—to see their fragmentation and rectify their weaknesses.

They started by targeting inpatient care. Their inaugural work delivered immediate benefits, especially heightened attention to taking small steps to minimize^ obstacles people encountered daily at the front lines. Figure 7.1 depicts that first cycle of discovery.

DISCOVERY CYCLE 2: DEEPEN UNDERSTANDING OF THE UNEXPECTED SITUATION

DeltaCare participants could have expected what people at many organizations would expect—that their new belief in obstacles as the problem would inevitably lead to targeted improvements by individuals in each unit. They didn't assume that either Correia or any other leader would have to guide further discovery. Removing the obstacles would put an end to the fragmentation in inpatient care flows.

But Correia was not satisfied with the output of one cycle of discovery. She recognized that the first cycle had provided only a top-level 60,000-foot view of the operational weaknesses that front-line people had to wrestle with. She wanted to gain deeper understanding of the challenge *in the context of implementing a solution*. That context was inpatient care—the area identified in the first cycle as "so broken."

Correia asked Maria Rodgers, the chief nursing officer (CNO), to kick off a second round of discovery. Rodgers set up events to map the specific flows of inpatient care. She invited clinicians, patients, the project manager, and Correia to participate. Rodgers onboarded new participants by invoking the surprising story of the earlier discoveries of fragmentation. The struggles of patients, she noted, obligated them to identify the obstacles to optimal inpatient care delivery.

Rodgers was taking the critical first step in a second round of discovery. She was updating new participants—and more generally updating new information to all. This updating, more than just a housekeeping exercise, heightened awareness of how the initiative's purpose originated, as well as how participants had so far evolved their beliefs.

Rodgers projected on the wall a fresh slide to map the flows for all to see. The group then filled in the services associated with current inpatient flow. By fleshing out the earlier maps, the group faced another surprise, and soon after, genuine doubt. That's because the new reality was far more unsettled than they thought. The task should have been straightforward for people who worked in inpatient care daily and lived with patients through their healthcare experience, but they struggled with it.

The project manager, Susan Walker, described what happened next:

> You knew things were broken. But then something happened that hits you in the gut so that you can't let go. It moves and compels you to do something different. It occurred when the hospital system president interjected, "I can see how the patients get into the hospital, but I can't see how they get out."

That remark provoked yet more surprise and many questions, notably: How could we *not know* how our patients get out of our system? Why are we having so much difficulty charting how patients move through the system from admission to discharge? Something wasn't making sense. In their confusion, however, they were on the cusp of benefiting from being deep in the second round of discovery, wrestling with their doubt about the viability of their persistent beliefs.

After wrestling with their questions, unable to harness doubt to further their understanding, they decided to switch focus. The new focus set aside their initial aim of better identifying obstacles. That approach wasn't contributing to progress. They decided instead to work the flows backward to admission and forward to discharge. This change of approach provoked an *aha* moment. It came when Rodgers turned the slide of the workflow map on its side. "We were taken aback," she said. "We realized, and then acutely realized at a different and deeper level, the old care process was oriented to justifying patient stay in the hospital."

Their willingness to engage with their surprise and genuine doubt helped them to discover something they had not seen before: *the care flow itself*—regardless of how accurately they mapped it—prevented patients from progressing seamlessly through their system. The delay in lab test results observed in the first discovery cycle was not just an obstacle but a dislocation in the system. They now knew they could not fix the system solely by removing care flow obstacles. They needed to redesign the whole process. A nurse manager explained the insight: "[optimal] Care is not driven by what the therapy can deliver, or when the physician can come.... That's a whole different paradigm shift ... it really requires us to be centered on the patient," not, as in most healthcare systems, on the institutional needs or physician schedules.

This experience challenged the belief born in the first round of discovery that they could improve inpatient care delivery solely by minimizing obstacles such as missed handoffs or workarounds to accommodate delayed scheduling of diagnostic tests. They needed to make a midcourse adjustment based on that *aha* moment: they needed to evolve their original purpose of minimizing care obstacles to one of creating a new model of care delivery that was truly patient driven. Figure 7.2 depicts this second cycle of discovery.

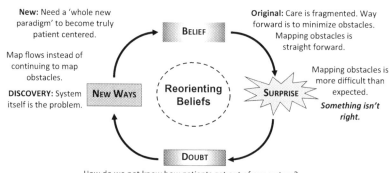

FIGURE 7.2 Deepen understanding of the unexpected situation.

You can see in the figure how a one-time cycle of discovery has limitations. It's beneficial but it often only gets sustainable transformation started. Multiple cycles deliver the ultimate prize. They spur insights and *ahas* that reorient a host of connected prior beliefs.

By engaging in multiple cycles, you are in a sense engaging in multiple acts of a play, each one advancing the plot and purpose of transformation. But each cycle does more than simply move a routine process ahead one step. Each one functions in a different way to help transform beliefs in a succession of mindset-reorganizing realizations.

You can see in the case of DeltaCare that both cycles 1 and 2 engaged and deepened everyone's understanding of the unsettled situation. They not only helped establish the purpose of the initiative, but they also helped evolve that purpose. The people at DeltaCare established as their initial purpose the minimization of obstacles, which helped them get started. But then, in cycle 2, as they bumped into unanticipated difficulties, they evolved that purpose to one of remaking the whole system.

DISCOVERY CYCLE 3: GENERATE FUTURE OBJECTS

The function of the third cycle of discovery in most organizations is to propel people to imagine a new future situation that promises to resolve the current unsettled one. As such, this act in the multipart play of discovery sits at a critical juncture between identifying the factors that make the current situation unsettled, which in turn clarifies the purpose of the transformation effort (cycles 1 and 2) and elaborating and negotiating the new practices and beliefs that might comprise that imagined future (cycles 4 and 5).

In DeltaCare, nursing leaders devoted several subsequent events to mapping key aspects of current care delivery. In one of them, Rodgers along with Walker assembled clinicians from various disciplines and current and former patients to examine the admissions process. Part of their work assessed whether clinicians effectively and efficiently collected data on incoming patients. This was an admission function clinicians believed was sound, which set the scene for surprise in the second cycle: They received considerable negative feedback from patients.

One patient noted that five different clinicians asked her the same question: "Why are you here?" Recounting the experience, she became frustrated—so frustrated that she looked directly at all the clinicians in the room and asked: "Why aren't you talking to each other?" A second patient jumped in and asked the clinicians if they understood "how aggravating it is to have different people ask you the same question as you lie helplessly in a strange bed." A third one hammered the point home: "Hold on. You all don't look like you know what you're doing. If you don't tell me that you know what you're doing, I won't think you do."

The clinicians, fielding patients' pointed questions, experienced surprise at its bluntest. That then moved them into genuine doubt, as they looked at each other and asked: "Are we failing to work together on care delivery? Could we be responsible for generating some of the confusion in care?" Sharing those experiences helped clinicians realize that they "weren't really acting together on such critical care." And that was a turning point during the third cycle, where they could genuinely harness doubt to their advantage.

Rather than dismissing the patients' feedback—which would have derailed discovery—the group persisted, using it to advance their transformation. They began to stop looking back to their old beliefs and practices, which had created such an unsettling situation in the first place, to gain their bearings and look forward toward imagining something new built on reoriented beliefs and practices. People *imagine forward*. This is the juncture that typifies cycle 3.

By *imagining forward*, they were loosening their hold on former experiences and generating discoveries about the future. At this point, the clinicians asked what would future patient care look like *if* they worked better together? What if they considered the concept a patient had suggested, "collaborative care"?

According to Walker, all agreed that the phrase brought forward an image of a concept that resonated with many of them: clinicians collaborating with each other and the patient at the bedside. That then became the concept—the future object—they imagined forward. The very idea opened new possibilities for consideration.

They did not commit to the idea at this point; they were just trying it on. As in other organizations that succeed with discovery, this was a time when the group held that image of the new future tentatively. They used it like a thought experiment, something to discard if it did not figure into their final resolution. In the meantime, it functioned to help the group transition away from prior belief (clinicians independently deliver care) and toward new ones, consistent with their imagined future.

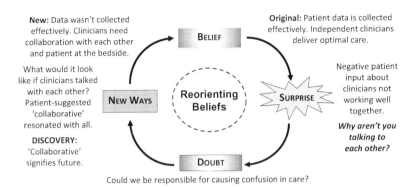

FIGURE 7.3 Generate future objects.

The patients' questions and stories had seeded a new belief: Patient-centered care demanded clinical teams that related to each other and to the patient at bedside from the time of admission to the time of discharge. Imagining a future object that aligned with that belief became yet another milestone in everyone's discovery journey. In a sense, it brought interim closure to act 3 in the organization's transformation. "That," said hospital president Correia, "was when the new care model was born." Figure 7.3 depicts their third cycle of discovery.

DISCOVERY CYCLE 4: ELABORATE NEW WAYS

You can see how cycle 3 leads naturally into cycle 4. That's when stakeholders build out and agree on what the imagined future looks like in practice. To do this, people imagine yet more possibilities that support the realization of the main one. DeltaCare managers and clinicians generated the "trio" concept to build out collaborative care.

The trio concept operationalized the idea of collaborative care, but then it invoked yet more surprise given that it would require clinicians to reorient beliefs and practices yet more. Clinicians did embrace the belief, developed in cycle 3, that they needed to collaborate with each other in the company of the patient at the bedside. However, they also believed that working together as a team—as a trio of nurse, pharmacist, and physician—would require intense, ongoing collaboration that was foreign to all of them. How, they wondered, would they be able to all appear at the same time, consistently in the patient's room? They had their doubts.

In the old world, said Sally Adams, the on-staff organization development (OD) specialist:

> Our providers [physicians] were used to going in . . . see the patient, come out, write orders, and the nurse tries to catch up; the pharmacist tries to catch up. But the new model requires . . . the team to assemble together in order to have the bedside care conference. And that causes them to practice differently. So . . . I don't want to say *sacrifice*, but it's changing how they practice and how they thought of themselves within that profession.

In the new world, clinicians would conduct the admitting assessment with the patient as a team. In turn, they would develop a single care plan. From then on, physician, nurse, and pharmacist would enter the patient's room together. Although the trio was nothing new for doctors, nurses, and pharmacists who often worked independently at arm's length, what was new was that they would now work arm in arm—*interacting as one* to deliver care. "The nurse isn't just standing by the door listening to the doctor, taking notes and orders," said a nurse. "The nurse participates in the physical exam and actively contributes to the discussion of orders and care plan."

Table 7.2 outlines the evolution of proposed new ways, including differences among clinician roles. You can see the scope of differences that you might aspire to in generating the transformation of any organization.

Doubt about the approach immediately crept in, however. The DeltaCare leaders understood the pending impact on clinicians and the need to support the clinicians' shift to being a trio. Correia expected the proposed new ways would "prompt clinicians to change their sense of what their profession is and their sense of who they are." The pharmacy director described it as a "complete role reversal" with pharmacists not on the sidelines of the action but as "active clinicians at the bedside."

The question for everyone was: Will the team of clinicians operate well in practice? The doctors, nurses, and pharmacists weren't sure. They expressed hesitancy. Their questions signaled just how much they would have to engage genuine doubt. How would they ask questions in front of the patient? What if they delegated work per the proposed new ways, but the other clinicians didn't follow through?

When they tried out the new approach, the doubts grew. Nurses admitted they had difficulty with aspects of their expanded role, in

TABLE 7.2 Evolution of Proposed New Ways Role and Expectation Change in DeltaCare's Discovery Process

	Move away from...	Move toward...	Proposed New Ways (Roles and Expectations)
Nurse	Doing bedside tasks. "Too much time spent running for supplies and equipment"	"Expanded and empowered role in decision making and patient-care progression. Responsible for bedside management of quality measures"	Work to full scope of practice. Trust other nurses to do the same. Listen to patient with team. Develop care plan.
Pharmacist	"Back-end role"	"Bedside presence" "Teacher to patient and clinical team"	Step out of backstage role. Interact with clinicians and patients. Listen to patient with team. Develop care plan.
Physician	Hierarchical orientation	"Partner in the care team who exposes her/his thinking to the professional team"	Listen to and consider the input of other clinicians, even in presence of a patient. Listen to patient with team. Develop care plan.

particular letting go of bedside tasks, such as administering medications. That, said one nurse, was "probably one of our biggest struggles." A pharmacist expressed his discomfort this way: "You now need to make sure ... the ball is not getting dropped some-where." Physicians too lamented a loss of control: "Where we struggle is the loss of control, some loss of autonomy, to a degree."

All clinicians acknowledged that involving patients in a real-time bedside conference was "definitely a role changer." How would they ask each other questions in front of the patient? How would they address patients' questions as a team? Physicians were especially uncomfortable in not knowing what to expect from the other clinicians:

> The other big change is having input from other clinicians. I want to say *challenged*.
>
> It's an adjustment to work as a team. Typically we're pretty autonomous, and we don't like to be told what to do. And now, all of a sudden, well, it's "You can't do it that way; we really need you to do it this way."
>
> Before, physicians were sort of independent. Now we have the nurse, the pharmacist, with us. I mean, we're all trained as physicians that we're going to work alone. And this is definitely more of being that "co" sort of thing.

These second thoughts are all part of the most productive part of the discovery cycle in trying on new ways. Anticipating difficulties with all clinicians, especially physicians, Rodgers, Walker, and Sally Adams, the organization development (OD) specialist, designed opportunities to practice the new ways before the new unit went live. Adams explained:

> It's not about just learning clinical processes. It's thinking differently about who they are as professionals within the context of that team delivering care. That doesn't happen just at the turn of a screw Everything in the current world will pull them back to the way they were functioning before . . . to do something differently really takes sustaining.

This period of trying on new ways prevented that from happening with clinicians. Going offsite, they mocked up a unit just like the imagined configuration that included patient rooms, servers, and central space. A nurse leader explained they would use the mockup for six weeks[3] of training and practice with volunteer patients so clinicians could "constantly experiment" and "unlearn old behaviors and learn new expectations."

For example, the new unit's nursing staff engaged in team-building exercises. With Adams, nursing staff explored how their roles and responsibilities would be different in the Collaborative Care model. In particular, they re-envisioned the nursing role as a partner with pharmacists and physicians. As Adams shared,

> This is a different challenge for nursing staff who may have perceived themselves in a more dependent role, as opposed to a

partner role with a pharmacist and physician to be able to give and receive feedback to other members of that professional team, especially if something is not going well.

Despite their early discomfort, clinicians valued the practice sessions. For them, the sessions helped to clarify the new clinical roles.

"Until you actually go and do it, you don't know what you don't know," said a pharmacist.

One physician commented: "Each [of us] needs to see it, feel it, touch it, give input on it, come to consensus . . . you can't just walk into one day."

Another physician, an early advocate, explained the value of the practice sessions: "So we came up with a theoretical process of how it was going to work. Trialing was incredibly important to say, 'OK, how does the flow actually work?'"

The mildly favorable physician response surprised Ann Green, the manager of physician engagement, who had expected disgruntlement from some of the physicians. Instead, having followed the cycle of discovery in a disciplined way, they were "pretty positive," offering comments such as, "Hey, this isn't so bad" and "I didn't see how this would work, but I can see how this can work now." Green also noticed that the physicians, by listening and asking questions, acted like "the pharmacist and nurse had something to add and contribute." She thought, "They might well become a team."

Clinicians were getting the opportunity to experience how they could actually operate as a trio. As a result, not only were physicians more positive than other group members had anticipated, but they discovered the trio works in practice. The six-week mockup offsite, including training with volunteers acting as real patients, boosted the launch. Moving away from prior beliefs about independence, clinicians generated the new belief that a multidisciplinary team of clinicians *can* effectively interact with the patient at the bedside. The practice may not have made the new process perfect, but it confirmed its practicality and potential.

Figure 7.4 depicts their fourth cycle of discovery.

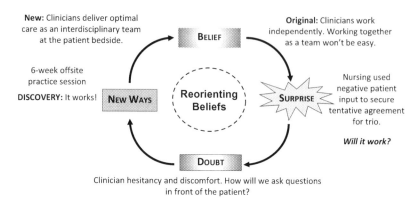

FIGURE 7.4 Elaborate new ways.

DISCOVERY CYCLE 5: NEGOTIATE NEW WAYS

The mockup and training set the stage for the final, fifth, act in the organization's transformation.

Cycle 5 in any organization features an effort by stakeholders to build out and agree on what the future object means in actual practice. Once again, they experience surprise right from the start as they try to manage the difficulties of implementation. That then leads to genuine doubt about the workability of their approach and renegotiation of terms that define it. If stakeholders agree with the new terms, everyone gets assurance that the product of their imaginations is viable. If not, the time comes to redesign, and if necessary, discard the new plan and go in a different direction.

Implementation of the new unit in DeltaCare progressed smoothly during the first few weeks. Clinicians and leaders knew the unit "was under the microscope of the whole organization, so everyone was trying to do the new process exactly." However, weeks 3 through 6 were difficult. This was the time, people said, when "things started to get really rough." They were once again confronted with surprise—the surprise from unexpected "bumps and bruises."

Thus began the next leg in their journey of discovery. Once it became apparent that rollout would require more attention, the hospital system president approved 90 additional days of support for the new unit. The project manager, OD specialist, and care improvement staff stayed on the unit to address emergent issues. They described their work as "purposeful watching" of the new care model in actual use. They observed backsliding:

> Doctors would start the bedside conference in the patient room without the nurse and pharmacist. Early on, you had a lot of that—doctors falling into their old patterns. So, we just kept working the care process deeper and deeper and deeper into the new patterns.

In caring for real patients, clinicians discovered areas needing more attention. For example, before going live with the new unit, nurses developed assigned stopping points or junctures in the care plan to evaluate the patient's progress to date. A group of nurses looked at how every task required for a patient's care connected with every other aspect of the patient's stay, such as timeliness of lab test results. But even as they addressed the flows so meticulously, they observed that the care flow was "*still* kind of disjointed" and "scattered."

This surprise prompted discussion about how to assure that what should happen for a patient did happen. Doubt over their procedures spurred some nurses to raise the idea of tollgates, a tool used in lean manufacturing—a checkpoint during which the project lead, sponsor, and stakeholders meet to review the progress of the project. To determine whether the tool would work in their situation, the nurses again listed all of the tasks that needed to be done for a patient. This time they ordered them by what needs to be done first versus the kind of activity that can be done second.

Arraying these tasks alongside every other aspect of a patient's stay, they realized, "Oh, [those junctures] could be our tollgates." As the clinical nurse leader said, "This is what needs to happen for this patient, in this amount of time. Only when we can say that's complete, can we move on. If it's not done, we're pulling the trigger."

Missed tollgates authorized nurses as the care manager to interrupt care progression and work with appropriate clinicians or ancillary services to solve the problem. For example, nurses can call the clinician team back to the bedside or follow up with ancillary services, such as lab orders, to avoid delay and needless trips for patients. As Correia put it: "Nurses are the keepers of the tollgates." As long as care is proceeding according to plan, the nurse advances the patient along the care pathway.

When initially proposed as a new practice to try on, tollgates provoked disagreement among physicians and between physicians and nurses. Physicians saw them as constraining their independence and authority. That probably stemmed in part from nurses describing the tollgates as a "must-do checklist," which they monitored "to the nth degree, because we were beginning a pilot."

But the tollgates also represented an unwelcome challenge to the prevailing belief in clinician independence. One physician even bluntly declared, "I really don't like this." Other physicians objected to having to drop what they were doing with patients on other units to return to the new unit. A typical question was: "Why would I come up and do a tollgate when I was just here two hours ago?" Physicians started to limit their use of tollgates.

Leaders were surprised by the physicians' challenge to the new approach. Green, the manager of physician engagement, noted how surprised she was that a few physicians "acted more on tilt" about tollgates, since they had not earlier fought its inclusion in collaborative care. On the other hand, one nursing manager admitted, "Basically, it [tollgates] just was not working." The full group moved into genuine doubt.

Walker then convened three events to hash out everyone's differences and search for a new solution that could be acceptable to everyone. The first two events yielded little progress. Green explained: the "first two whacks at it . . . was just like an impasse." The physicians shared a few ideas, she said, but the "originators of the unit, the real strong nursing champions, became exasperated that the physicians didn't get it. And then the physicians got frustrated that others didn't get *them*." They ventured deeper into genuine doubt.

During the third event, a "breakthrough," or *aha* moment, finally occurred. The OD and care facilitators presented data showing that, when physicians participated in tollgates, "even if it was begrudgingly," post-discharge statistics were more favorable. The data were really dramatic. There was no misunderstanding them. They discovered that tollgates really did improve care.

Following on the breakthrough moment, clinicians agreed to negotiated changes that made tollgates "less arbitrary" for physicians. These changes also allowed nursing to "own more of the process," calling in physicians only when "absolutely necessary." For this arrangement to work, physicians would need to specify milestones that a patient should reach at particular points. Nursing would monitor those

AMPLIFYING DISCOVERY

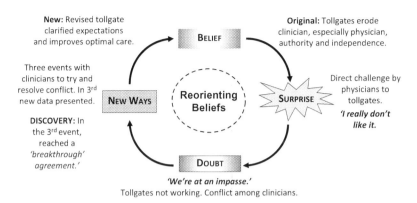

FIGURE 7.5 Negotiate new ways.

points and assess whether to call in the physician. Physicians were also expected to return to the unit at designated intervals. Walker commented: "Basically, it was clearer to both physicians and nurses what the expectations were." Green summarized, "It was almost a compromise, but it was a realistic compromise that people could do."

Figure 7.5 depicts their fifth cycle of discovery.

Their negotiation of terms led to the discovery that when physicians abided by tollgates, care improved. They reached a new agreement that adjusted this new element of the model, changing and clarifying expectations. By keeping the new element of tollgates, but revising its terms, clinicians refined their belief about independence, while continuing to hold the new belief of relating as a team in care delivery. The beliefs and practices embedded in the new model regained the assurance necessary to continue in operation.

The new model was well received. Getting positive feedback from patients and families helped the clinicians—especially the physicians and pharmacists—to get more comfortable with the new model. It also enabled everyone in DeltaCare to discover what a positive difference the new model made for patient care. The new model yielded superior care metrics. Leaders came from around the world to learn the secret of DeltaCare's model. News reports captured some of the visitors' comments; about how different the model was from "99.5%" of US healthcare delivery; and the "guts" it took to question the tenet that physicians give orders and nurses implement them.

A few years after introducing the new model, clinicians describe the impact on roles and interactions with patients.

It not only helps in patient care; it helps in staff care. It works. It really works. (Physician)

I've seen both sides of the world . . . the difference is collaborative care is a functional unit. There's better communication with staff. The patient has a better experience. People aren't coming in and out a million times . . . the mindset basically is we all have a goal and it's to get the patient the best care that they need. (Clinical Nurse Assistant)

I really like this opportunity to interact on the front end with other medical professionals and have more interaction with the patients. (Pharmacist)

SUMMARY

DeltaCare's story shows that bringing the process of discovery to an end after one engagement of the three motors can short-circuit successful transformation. In fact, it shows that you should never bring the *possibility* of discovery to a stop. Only by making the discovery process continuous can stakeholders fully discover how to transform a system most effectively—as evidenced in the example of DeltaCare's new care model. You need to connect one cycle to another, developing a set of five (or more) escalating cycles of growth and insight to deliver success. With the unique benefits of each of the five cycles, you tap discovery at its highest potential, integrating it into all parts of understanding and resolving the puzzling situation, and reinforcing the multiple discoveries generated in each of the cycles.

Correia set the example. She championed and supported clinicians, leaders, and other stakeholders in all five discovery cycles. She meanwhile took part in some of the events and contributed to the efforts. To begin, she and her leadership, clinicians, and other stakeholders advanced their understanding of the puzzling mapping difficulties. As a next step, they deepened their understanding of that situation by exploring the specifics of inpatient care flows, which helped them realize they needed to evolve their purpose. In the third cycle of discovery, they surfaced an image—what became the future of collaborative care—that resonated with everyone's aspirations for care quality. In the fourth, they built out that image with the concept of a trio of clinicians at patients' bedsides. And in the fifth cycle, they built out and renegotiated the terms of tollgates and reoriented their beliefs to support it.

You can see how much more powerful multiple cycles of discovery are compared to a one-off exercise. Discovery is an always-possible exercise, not just a tool to pull out now and again to address a single issue. Its benefits pile up with each cycle, as people regularly confront and work through surprise, genuine doubt, and launching new ways. The next chapter, chapter 8, brings the book to a close by exploring the larger potential impact of discovery processes on reorienting prevailing beliefs and practices of change management.

~~~~~

1. Think of a successful change-management process in your organization. What contributed to its success? Was it a one-time change effort or the result of a continuous and ongoing effort? What were its hallmarks? Which of the discovery cycles were most relevant in your process?
2. What does it look like to *imagine forward?* How could you integrate imagining forward into your work with others that would generate future objects?
3. How are the benefits of discovery compounded over multiple cycles? What stands to be gained from taking an always-possible approach to discovery?

NOTES

1 The data and charts for the DeltaCare case are based on the article: Golden-Biddle, Karen A. 2020. "Discovery as Abductive Mechanism for Reorienting Habits within Organizational Change." *Academy of Management Journal* 63(6):1951–1975. They are being used with the permission of the Academy of Management.
2 With the exception of hospital system president, Kathryn Correia, the names of the DeltaCare organization and staff used in this chapter are pseudonyms.
3 Nurses selected to staff the initial unit were released from usual clinical responsibilities for much of the training period to familiarize themselves with the new clinical processes, physical layout, and technology and to make final adjustments. Two weeks were allocated for cross clinical training with physicians and pharmacists. During joint sessions, clinical teams practiced delivering care as a trio to volunteer patients.

REFERENCE

Golden-Biddle, Karen A. 2020. "Discovery as Abductive Mechanism for Reorienting Habits within Organizational Change." *Academy of Management Journal* 63(6):1951–1975.

8 Discovery's Impact on Change Management

The leaders and group members in the stories highlighted throughout this book didn't just discover something new. During their work together, they transformed nebulous, puzzling, and sometimes arduous situations, all the while undergoing their own transformations. After his team at General Electric redesigned their MRI, Doug Dietz became design lead. He is still known and highly regarded for his advocacy work, integrating empathy into design.

A nurse in DeltaCare underwent a similar transformation. When confronting challenging situations that upended her beliefs, she and the other group members engaged in the discovery process catalyzed new ways of operating that made a positive difference. "It took," she said, "17 to 18 years for me to become the nurse I've always wanted to be. Very strongly do I feel this model is the right thing for our patients and for me professionally."

Given the 85 percent failure rate of cultural change in most organizations, these stories are remarkable examples of success. These leaders beat the odds, but they did more than that. By succeeding through embracing the discovery process, they and their colleagues took a path that goes beyond familiar change-management practices—and far beyond the limited scope and assumptions of change management as still taught in North American business schools.

What is so different about discovery? Three factors bring to life the discovery process in ways that traditional change management does not.

DOI: 10.4324/9781003513681-9

STARTING FROM A DIFFERENT PLACE

Change management traditionally begins with a preset *problem*. If you're involved in these efforts, no matter whether your role is as a leader or employee, someone before you has probably defined the problem and designated its solution. You're not asked to question your beliefs about either the problem (is that the real problem?) or solution (will it work in practice?). Nor does anyone suggest that further exploration is necessary.

When the time comes to launch change, you then wait either for the proposed change to reach your unit or until you are officially tasked to help facilitate others' adoption of that change. You're not brought in until after the moment when you could have had the most impact.

If you engage in the discovery process, you're brought in earlier. You're asked to join with others to try and make sense of an indeterminate or vague *situation*. Wrestling with the situation, not a defined problem, makes a world of difference. You start by actively engaging the situation to discover what you don't know. You don't assume to know the problem. You don't yet know—and won't for a while—what kind of solution you and the rest of the group will create to address the situation.

By leaving your office and immersing yourself in a situation, you increase the odds of deepening your understanding. You take part in clearing up the situation's cloudiness. You define what's problematic about that situation before defining the problem to be solved. Starting from difficult or nebulous situations highlights the messiness, emotions, turbulence, and struggles we all experience in dealing with a new reality. Life is anything but straightforward. And certainly, it is not linear.

Starting from this different place—the situation, not a problem—obligates you to see the new reality and confront the challenge in all its complexity. Everyone, together with others, experiences what they *don't* yet know. This is how change management conducted with a discovery process provides the opportunity to recognize and incorporate the unsettling nature of unexpected situations—and benefit from the creativity that comes from the genuine doubt that follows. The human emotions that accompany change fuel new ideas that transform the situation.

ACCESSING EXPERIENCE

Change management also typically aims to *gain the users' acceptance* of the designated solution. Let's suppose we are talking about a solution that comes in the form of software. The ultimate goal of the change effort is to get the software solution adopted by all those who will need to use it. Project leaders typically follow a change methodology that prescribes sequences of steps to organize and implement efforts that assure the right people adopt the solution. They reach out to individuals who are late in adopting the software to help convince them of the reasons to come on board.

By contrast, change management using the discovery process aims to *access the users' experience*[1] as part of exploring the unsettled situation. The ultimate goal of each round of the discovery process—for the leaders and group members as well as those impacted by the pending change—is to reorient their beliefs. With that reorientation, people naturally drive to reject practices that no longer work in light of the new situation.

Traditional change management addresses how to bring about the users' acceptance of the new software. Change management done through the discovery process instead addresses how to access the experience of the users. The "walking with" exercise discussed in chapter 5 highlights this difference. So does inviting some users to become members of the discovery group.

You can see how the process of discovery stems from a very different belief about how change occurs. Gaining the users' acceptance of a solution highlights the belief that change occurs by convincing people. It focuses on providing information that will help people understand why the solution is good for them to adopt. Accessing experience, on the other hand, highlights the belief that change occurs by surfacing and reflecting on people's perceptions, struggles, joys, and challenges as part of getting to know what you don't know about the unsettled situation.

TREATING DISCOVERY AS CONTINUOUS

Traditionally, change management assumes that planning and design (including selection of the solution) occurs first. Implementation then follows. Planning and implementation are considered separate and sequential functions, usually delegated to different sets of people. Business schools, for example, offer separate courses covering strategy formulation and strategy implementation. In business organizations more generally, leaders form separate design and implementation teams, again with different people on each.

When you lead a discovery process, in contrast, you recognize planning and implementation activity, but assume no sharp distinction in the sequencing between them. You iteratively adjust each one as needed throughout the process, one continuously influencing the other. Indeed, the goal of creating something new, central to the discovery process, assumes that new beliefs and practices come during both planning and implementation. That's what happened at Delta-Care (chapters 2 and 7), Microsoft (chapters 2 and 3), and Canlis (chapter 4). Everyone involved took part in design and implementation.

Traditional change management also assumes that discovery as an event happens only at certain times, in particular only in the earliest phase of the change process. It happens when innovators, designers, or planners—often disconnected from users—generate the solution to the problem. This discrete view of discovery as a time-locked event reinforces the sharp separation between planning and implementation in change management. People who will execute the solution are isolated from its creation and have very little knowledge about why and how the solution came to be.

And that in turn drives the need to gain acceptance of a solution only after its creation. The result is that this taken-for-granted belief of isolating people also suppresses the discovery of ways to refine, challenge, validate, or question the suitability of the solution in practice. When you use the discovery process, in contrast, you view discovery as continuously occurring in the change process, throughout and beyond implementation. Indeed, as my research[2] shows, it potentially happens at all times. The boundary between planning and implementation efforts is not so distinct and impermeable as many leaders think.

If a view of the discovery process as continuous were incorporated into the practice of most organizations' change-management practices, it could reshape the purpose and the trajectory of the change, as well as alter how and when people become involved. The change process would better position people to design a solution suited to the particular context of its use. It could also mitigate hurdles that crop up from unexpected glitches during implementation because discovery would become an expectation of implementation, not a surprising afterthought.

IS A DISCOVERY PROCESS CALLED FOR?

The particular power of the discovery process, in contrast to traditional change management, is that it paves the way for people to let go of beliefs that no longer guide successful behavior and embrace new ones that better fit the new circumstances. Currently, the practice of traditional change management does not have much success in driving change that requires core belief change. Integrating the discovery process into traditional change management helps alleviate this weakness.

As a practical matter, leaders face a choice with the advent of new realities or unexpected situations. They must differentiate change that requires new beliefs and practices—reimagining, rethinking, redesigning work—from change that requires only minor adjustments to practices, and no belief change of significance to those impacted.

How do you evaluate if you should use the discovery process? You need to address the question: *Does the unexpected situation demand belief change in your organization?* The answer depends on whether the situation is not only unexpected, but also calls into question core prevailing ways of operating in your organization.

Rather than suppressing what you don't know about the situation, you start a discovery process focused on finding out more about it. That's what NBA Commissioner Adam Silver did in March 2020. He had already been using the discovery enabler (chapter 3), seeking clues about a possible virus. He canvassed experts about its potential and solicited opinions from league owners and other stakeholders on how they might proceed. His early search for clues yielded information that helped NBA leadership act quickly when the time came. On the day that the World Health Organization declared the coronavirus a global pandemic and the first NBA player tested positive, the NBA became the first sports league to temporarily suspend its remaining season.

That kind of proactive success comes only when you're watching for clues inherent in unexpected situations to help you evaluate whether your organization's beliefs could be in question and demand change. Clues can be obvious, such as negative employee feedback, although even obvious ones can be ignored. Alternatively, clues can be too-easily-disregarded hints or gut feelings that something is awry, such as unusual pauses of silence in conversations. Both types of clues are important. It's up to you to draw attention to these clues and use them to both strengthen everyone's understanding and shape follow-on efforts.

The stories in this book show how an approach featuring the discovery processes catalyzed leaders' actions when situations demanded belief change in their organizations—and often their own. These stories reveal the positive impact that can result when discovery processes are integrated into change management. If you do decide that only through discovery's benefits will your change management succeed, then you'll need the skills of a leader of people such as Doug Dietz, Satya Nadella, Kathryn Correia, and others in this book.

How did they lead in ways that furthered belief change through discovery? These leaders share a repertoire or toolkit comprised of skills and behaviors that set them apart from those who suppress discovery. See Table 8.1 for a chart comparing the skills and behaviors of suppression and discovery leaders.

The first skill is practicing belief flexibility—the letting go of ill-fitting beliefs and taking up new ones. Belief flexibility is foundational because discovering anything new requires us to change at least one of our core beliefs. The leaders consistently modelled and supported others in the practice of belief flexibility.

The second is progressing the discovery cycles. A process like discovery—patterned, flexibly implemented, and iterative—requires that discovery leaders know how to *progress* the discovery cycles, not stifle them with control and the use of derailers. A key question to ask in determining and facilitating group progress is: What is the next best step to take, in light of progress with the cycle?

The third skill is leading with confident humility. Although humility and confidence may seem like odd partners, leading with both enables you to create optimal combinations of belief and doubt for discovery. In chapter 4, we explored Adam Grant's diagram, the confidence sweet spot. You exude confidence as a leader. And *at the same time*, you express humility.

The fourth is a set of behaviors—discovery enablers. Together with the three skills, these behaviors position discovery leaders to work with others to cultivate discovery and deliver meaningful new ways of working and relating, consistently and genuinely.

TABLE 8.1 Comparing the Skills and Behaviors of Suppression and Discovery Leaders

Suppression Leader	Discovery Leader
Maintains belief rigidity Hold beliefs tightly. Starts with a pre-defined problem.	**Practices belief flexibility** Loosen hold of beliefs, take up new ones. Starts with a problematic situation.
Stifles discovery cycles Stay the course. Avoid challenges to beliefs and practices.	**Progresses discovery cycles** Remain flexible and attentive. Explore challenges to beliefs and practices.
Leads with overconfidence Believe without doubt. Certain and all knowing.	**Leads with confident humility** Seek the "confidence sweet spot." Vulnerable to not knowing.
Leads with discovery derailers Ignores Unsettling Clues. Explains Away Discrepancies. Censors Contrary Ideas.	**Leads with discovery enablers** Capitalizes on Surprise Savor surprise. Seek clues to surprise. Set surprise in motion. Harnesses Genuine Doubt Ask questions from a discovery mindset. Strike a balance of belief and doubt. Inject doubt to mitigate overconfidence. • *Explicitly consider unknowns.* • *Say "I don't know" honestly.* • *Create learning culture oriented to discovery.* Inject beliefs to mitigate debilitating doubt. • *Doubt tools, not self.* • *Generate small wins.* • *Invoke meaningful keep focus on mission, purpose, values.* Deploy hypothetical entities.
Builds Capacity for Executing Traditional Change Narrow team to "experts." Presume no up-front employee engagement. Support division of labor and thinking. **Potential transition to discovery approach** Respond to discovery wake-up call.	Launches New Ways Sees beyond expectations. • *Use "walking with" exercise.* Permit and enables recombination. Assess suitability of new ways. Builds Capacity for Discovery Build diverse representation. Foster respectful engagement. Design flexibility into roles.

The ultimate goal of your personal development is to become a guide of continuous discovery cycles, in which you and your colleagues power novel solutions to unexpected situations and new realities that upend beliefs. That's the new imperative. That's how you have an impact that matters. An impact that strengthens communities and organizations. An impact that builds capacity to guide and support discovery on your team or in your organization. That's how you will have a noteworthy impact on your personal growth, whether at work or in life.

~~~~~

1. Identify a recent change-management initiative in your organization that should have incorporated a discovery process but did not. If you could restart it, how would you explain to colleagues the need to integrate a discovery process? What would be your first step to integrate one?
2. Review both columns of Table 8.1. Identify the skills and behaviors you currently use. Reflect on your list. Which would you like to further strengthen? Which do you want to change?
3. On Table 8.1, identify one skill or behavior from the "Discovery Leader" column. What small actions will you implement in the next week to develop your selection and enrich your personal capacity for leading discovery?

NOTES

1 This sub-section is inspired by the work of Mary Parker Follett. Follett, Mary Parker. 2013 (1951). *Creative Experience*. Mansfield Centre, CT: Martino Publishing, p. 200.
2 Golden-Biddle, Karen A. 2020. "Discovery as Abductive Mechanism for Reorienting Habits of Belief and Practice within Organizational Change." *Academy of Management Journal* 63(6):1951–1975.

REFERENCES

Follett, Mary Parker. 2013 (1951). *Creative Experience*. Mansfield Centre, CT: Martino Publishing.
Golden-Biddle, Karen A. 2020. "Discovery as Abductive Mechanism for Reorienting Habits within Organizational Change." *Academy of Management Journal* 63(6):1951–1975.

Index

Page numbers in *italics* indicate figures; page numbers in **bold** indicate tables.

action, situated: importance of 4, 84–86, 94, accessing experience 138; starting from a different place 137
Ain, Aron 56–57
Alon, Uri 72–73
amplifying discovery, *see* discovery cycles, multiple for amplification
asking questions from a discovery mindset 69–70
Argyris, Chris 17
Austin, Robert 52

belief, beliefs: as habits of expectation 31–32, 40, 42n15, 88; expectations, seeing beyond 87–90; flexibility of 32–33, 49–51, 111, **118–119**; rigidity of 25, 31, 37, 41, 53, 65, **74**
belief change 1–5, 31, 48, 65, 140–141; moving away from past patterns 33–37; moving toward new patterns 37–40; reorienting belief through discovery process 31–32, *33*; *see also* discovery, process of and discovery cycle, basic
Bernard, Claude 62, 65
Boorstin, Daniel 71
Boston Healthcare for the Homeless Program 82, 95n1
British Royal Infirmary (BRI): discovery suppression 16–17, 71, 89

Brooks, George 17–18
building capacity for discovery 99–111: relational nature of discovery 102; building diverse representation 103–104; designing flexibility into roles 108–110; fostering respectful engagement 104–108, *107*; skills and behaviors of discovery leaders for 140–143, **142**
Burris, Ethan 19

Canlis 62–68, 70, 74–76, 85, 94, 139; founding of 77n1
Canlis, Brian 62, 64, 67, 75
Canlis, Mark 62–63, 67, 75
capacity for discovery, *see* building capacity for discovery
capitalizing on surprise, enablers: savoring surprise 53–54; seeking clues to surprise 55–56; setting surprise in motion 56–57; skills and behaviors of discovery leaders for 140–143, **142**; *see also* surprise
Carmeli, Abraham 105
Carroll, Patrick 73
Carter, Jimmy 100, 104–106
Carter Center, The 100–102: eradication program 101, 103–104, 112n12, 114n40; reported cases of Guinea worm disease 101, 112n3

146　INDEX

Case, Jean 21–22, 24n15, 25n37
Case, Steve 24n13
Case Foundation 9–11, 21–23, 24n13; PlayPump International-US (PPI) 10, 21; US government and 9–10
censoring contrary ideas, *see* discovery suppression
Centers for Disease Control and Prevention (CDC); Guinea Worm Disease Eradication Program 100–101; West Nile virus and St. Louis encephalitis 69
Chabris, Christopher 88
Chai, Sen 15
change management: accessing experience 138; comparing skills and behaviors of suppression and discovery leaders **142**; contribution of discovery process to change 140–143; discovery as continuous throughout change 138–140; starting from a different place 137
clues, response to 14–15, 19, 21–22, 49, 51, 55–57, 140–141
cognitive bias 79n19
confidence sweet spot, the **74**
confident humility 73, **74**
Cook, Scott 53–54
Correia, Kathryn 33–34, 39–41, 42n18, 56, 104, 117, 120–121, 125–126, 131, 134, 141
culture, creating a discovery-oriented 28–31, 72–73

DeltaCare 102, 111, 136, 42n18, 43n19–21, 135n1–3: diverse stakeholders 104; expectations 87; discovery cycles, full set **118–119**; evolution of proposed new roles and expectations, **127**; mapping care flows 34–37, 55, 94; walking with exercise, 87–90, 138
Detert, James 19
Devin, Lee 52
Dietz, Doug 45–50, 55–56, 66–68, 85–86, 91, 136, 141
discovery as process 1–3, 28–31: belief flexibility 32–33, 49–51, 54–55, 57, 70, 90, 92, 103; building capacity for 99–111, *107*; compels a special reasoning of abductive logic 49, 59n5; constrained view of 12–14; continuous process 32, 138–140; evolving purpose through 74–75; invitation to 6–7; relational nature of 102; reorienting belief through 31–32, *33*; story of 40–41
discovery, basic cycle 5, 32, *33*, *35*: capitalizing on surprise 45–58, *48*: harnessing genuine doubt 62–77, *66*; launching new ways 82–95, *85*; three motors 1–3
discovery cycles, in stories depicted: creating new ways of delivering patient care 33–41, 117–134, 43n19; *35, 120, 122, 125,* **127**, *130, 133,* **118–119**; redesigning an MRI machine 45–48, *48, 50,* 55–56; redesigning core ways of operating during a crisis 62–68, 74–76, *66*; rethinking what it means to be a doctor 82–85, 89, 92–94, *85*; generating new ways to treat a centuries-old disease 99–111, *107*
discovery cycles, multiple for amplification 95, **118–119**, 134–135: deepen understanding of the unexpected situation 120–123, *122*; elaborate new ways 125–130, **127**, *130*; engage the unexpected situation 117–120, *120*; generate future objects 123–125, *125*; negotiate new ways 130–134, *133*
discovery, leadership: comparing skills and behaviors of discovery and suppression leaders 140–143, **142**
discovery mindset 51; asking questions from 69–70
discovery motors **142**; capitalizing on surprise 45–58; harnessing genuine doubt 62–77; launching new ways 82–95, *see also* discovery cycle, basic.
discovery suppression: belief rigidity 31, 37, 41, 47, 49, 53–54, 65, 70–71, 90; negative consequences of 3,

5, 14, 32, 67, 70, 76; constrained view of discovery 12–14; discovery derailers 14–23; censoring contrary ideas 18–21, 31–32; explaining away discrepancies 16–18; ignoring unsettling clues 14–15; skills and behaviors of suppression leaders **142**; treat as a helpful wake-up call 21–23
doubt, debilitating 73, **74**; *see also* genuine doubt and harnessing genuine doubt
Dougherty, Deborah 55
dracunculias 99, 111n2; also known as Guinea worm disease (GWD) 106–107
Drew, Trafton 88–89
Dunne, Danielle 55
Duras, Marguerite 89
Dutton, Jane 105
Dweck, Carol 29

empathic listening 105–106
engagement, respectful 104–108
expectations, seeing beyond your 87–90
experience: accessing experience of those potentially impacted 50, 55, 90, 138; as eye-opening 38, 46; clash with beliefs 48, 122; exposure to different 90–92, 94, 103
explain away discrepancies, *see* discovery suppression

fallibility of knowing 71, 73: explicitly consider unknowns 71–72; say "I don't know" honestly 72
Fernbach, Philip 71
Field, Joris 53
Field, Trevor 8–10, 13
flexibility of belief, *see* discovery as process, belief flexibility
Foege, William 100
Follett, Mary Parker 143n1
Fox, Craig 71
Frontline (television show) 9
future objects, generating 123–125

General Electric Healthcare Innovation Lab 45, 50, 136

genuine doubt 66–68: as source of inventiveness 68; different than self-doubt or skepticism 66; doubt your tools, not yourself 73–74. **74**; doubtful energy 67–68; emotion 72–73; fallibility of knowing 71; importance of not knowing 2, 29, 65, 76; culture supportive of 72–73; nature of 66–68; no genuine doubting of beliefs, no discovery; term of Charles Peirce 66, *see also* harnessing genuine doubt
Goncalo, Jack 14
Grant, Adam 73, **74**, 141
growth mindset, concept of Dweck 29, 42n4

Hacking, Ian 18
Hardin, Ashley 105
harnessing genuine doubt, enablers: as second motor to engage what is not known 68; harnessing 62–77; asking questions from a discovery mindset 69–70; deploying hypothetical entities 75–76; striking a balance of belief and doubt 70–75; injecting doubt to mitigate overconfident knowing 71–73, **71**; injecting belief to mitigate debilitating doubt 73–75; skills and behaviors of discovery leaders for 140–143, **142**
Hogan, Kathleen 30
Hopkins, Donald 100–102, 104–106, 110
hypothetical entities, *see* harnessing genuine doubt

"Icarus Paradox," (term) 90
ignore unsettling clues, *see* discovery suppression
Inc. (magazine) 54
International Drinking Water Supply and Sanitation Decade (IDWSSD) 100
Intuit 53, 106

Jobs, Steve 92

Kaiser Family Foundation 9
Klein, Gary 19–20

Kreuter, Marshall 102, 109
Kronos (now ÜKG) 56–57
Kuhn, Thomas 17

Lamott, Anne 90
launching new ways, enablers: as third motor to generate desired new practices and beliefs 83–86; seeing beyond your expectations 87–90; permitting recombination 90–92; assessing suitability of new ways 92–94; skills and behaviors of discovery leaders for 140–143, **142**
LifeStraw® 110
Leonardi, Paul 76

Mandela, Nelson 9
mapping, care flows 34–37
Massachusetts Department of Health: funding of medical van 93
McInnis, Barbara 82–85, 89
Melwani, Shimul 14
Microsoft Corporation 28–31, 41, 51, 57, 70, 91, 102, 139
Miller, Danny 90
mission, purpose, and values, invoking 74–75
Mueller, Jennifer 14
Munson, Dave 93

Nadella, Satya 28–31, 41, 57, 90–91, 141
National Basketball Association (NBA) 140
new ways, launching 82–84, 85, 94–95, **142**: emotion 72–73, 104–105; overcomes selective attention 89; prioritizes local and frontline action 84; suitability 92–94; "walking with" exercise 87–90, 138, **142**
New York Times, The (newspaper) 28
New York University, Development Research Institute 22

O'Connell, James 82–85, 89, 92–94
overconfidence 71–73

Peirce, Charles 42n14, 66, 69
Pin, Chew Lock 19

Pine Street Inn 82–85, 89, 93–94
PlayPump: alliance 9–10; Case Foundation rethinks involvement with 21; collaboration ignores clues 15; constrained view of discovery 12–14; UNICEF and Skat Consulting Ltd evaluations of PlayPump installation 10–11
Poincaré, Henri 70
Pragmatism 78n11: experience 143; starting of any question as indicator of doubt 69; genuine doubt 66; habit as disposition to act 42n15, *see also* Peirce, Charles and Follett, Mary Parker

Rankin, Amy 53
Red Hat 72
recombination for discovery 90–92
relational nature of discovery 102
reorienting belief, *see* belief change
representation, diverse 103–104
respectful engagement 104–108
rigidity of belief, *see* discovery suppression, belief rigidity
role flexibility, designing 108–110
Roundabout Outdoors, South Africa 9–11; installing PlayPump 10
Ruiz-Tiben, Ernesto 101, 104

saying "I don't know" honestly 72
self-doubt, 66, 73, **74**, **142**; *see also* genuine doubt
Shanley, John Patrick 68
scientific discovery, research: new drug development 55; normal science 18; lactic acid 17–18; near misses 15
Silver, Adam 140
Simons, Daniel 88
situated action, *see* action, situated
Sloman, Steven 71
small wins, to inject confidence 74
Snowden, David 19
Socrates 69
South African Department of Water Affairs and Forestry 9
special reasoning 49, 59n5

stories: of discovery 40–41; selection of 3–4; and surprise 49–50
striking a balance of belief and doubt 70–55
Structure of Scientific Revolutions, The (Kuhn) 17
Stuyver, Ronnie 8–9, 13
Sullivan, Erin 52
surprise, capitalizing on 45–58: as discovery's first motor 47–51, *48*; compels a special reasoning 49, 59n5; emotion 72–73, 105; gives rise to a new story 49–51; insists on flexibility 51; 'no surprise' management 52; study of pilot experiences of surprise during flight 53

Taylorism 13, 24n17
Teh, Cheryl Ann 19
Think Again (Grant) 73, **74**
Tuareg people, invention of new way to filter water to protect against Guinea worm disease 109–110

United Kingdom (UK), National Health Service 16
United Nations 99–100
United Nations Children's Fund 100
unknowns, explicitly consider 71–72
users' experience, access 138

Vestergaard 110
Võ, Melissa 88–89

wake-up call, treat discovery derailers as 21–23; *see also* discovery suppression
"walking with" exercise 87–90, 138, **142**
Walters, Daniel 71
Water for People 22
Whitehurst, James 72
Whittinghill, Joe 30
Wolfe, Jeremy 88–89
Woltjer, Rogier 53
World Health Organization 100, 140

Printed in the United States
by Baker & Taylor Publisher Services